# CONTENTS

112446

# ECUMENISM—
## A MOVEMENT TOWARD
## CHURCH UNITY

## William G. Rusch

FORTRESS PRESS        PHILADELPHIA

*In Memoriam*

My parents

F. L. Cross

M. G. H. Gelsinger

C. E. Prater

who in their own ways taught me
about the unity of the church

**Library of Congress Cataloging in Publication Data**

Rusch, William G.
   Ecumenism : a movement toward church unity.

   1. Christian union.   2. Ecumenical movement.
I. Title.
BX8.2.R84   1985      270.8′2      84-48707
IBSN 0–8006–1847–5

1253J84   Printed in the United States of America   1–1847

# FOREWORD

Many believe that "the hinge of history" is opening the door to a totally new ecclesiastical era. The possibilities for that era's unfolding are intriguing, particularly in the light of the divisions that exist within the church of Jesus Christ. Will those divisions be of less significance in the century ahead? Will Christians be more tolerant of one another and of the diverse patterns of theology, worship, and church practice than has been true for the last 450 years? Is it possible that the ancient breach between Eastern and Western Christendom will be healed? Will Protestants and Roman Catholics be reconciled? Will Christians find new expressions of fellowship, of communion, with one another?

These are fascinating questions, questions to which some of us dare to hope for positive answers. We are firmly convinced that Jesus Christ intends oneness to exist among his people; whatever destroys that oneness is contrary to his will. We have dared to envision a possible visible expression of the "one, holy, catholic, and apostolic church," based soundly on careful study of the New Testament and appropriately consonant with the confessions by which we have learned to articulate the faith of the church and which we hold individually.

In the Lutheran Church in America—as in other church bodies—that vision has been profound and directive. The responsible search for ways of expressing the unity that is given us in Christ not only has a long history but also has been labeled among the highest priorities that we seek to implement today. We cannot conceive of a denomination's existence apart from other denominations, nor Christians assuming that their destinies diverge from those of other Christians.

Thus we are committed firmly to the ecumenical movement in its many manifestations. We were a part of the councils of churches from their very beginning. We have also experienced the deep satisfaction of theological dialogues which have resulted in converging strains of thought and which at times have been able to state theological consensus.

Since 1979, when he became director for Ecumenical Relations within the Division for World Mission and Ecumenism, William G. Rusch has fulfilled a central role within the Lutheran Church in America in the programmatic expression of its concern for unity. He and I have traveled together to many parts of the world to assure other church leaders of the genuineness of the Lutheran Church in America's statement and of our intention to implement it. Over and over again we have been awestruck by our visits to places where we have found openness, fellowship, agreement, faith, and understanding far beyond our hopes and expectations.

We have asked the question many times, "How can we share what we are experiencing?" After all, the unity of the church must be expressed in all dimensions of the church's life and witness. How can people in congregations in Omaha, Nebraska; Seattle, Washington; Seguin, Texas; Miami, Florida; Hickory, North Carolina; or Syracuse, New York be informed of what is taking place and share in its excitement? None of us wants to be left behind when history is moving ahead.

Thus, many times I urged Dr. Rusch to write a book stating the theological basis for our task and a brief history of what has transpired. Here is the result. I am delighted to commend this book to what I hope will be its many readers. These pages depict a pilgrimage, a road to an envisioned goal, to which the reader is invited to come along.

One caution—the ecumenical literature is extensive and diversified. This book is, in a genuine sense, only an outline. Many readers will want to explore the source materials that are described here. There is a syllabus contained within these covers for quite a theological education.

A final word of appreciation—to the Lutheran Church in America for its firm commitment to the unity of the church, to the various divisions and committees that have taken the task to heart and have drafted documents for consideration for the "highest legislative authorities," to the church's Executive Council, to its conventions for responsible action, and to individuals too numerous to mention who have been a part of all that is described in these pages.

And to William G. Rusch, renowned scholar in the patristic period of the church's history, a man of deep personal faith and commitment to the gospel, a Lutheran of great confessional integrity as well as an ecumenist of profound persuasion, above all—a colleague and friend in pilgrimage. Thanks be to God for your partnership in the gospel of our Lord Jesus Christ.

Advent 1984

JAMES R. CRUMLEY, JR.
*Bishop*

# PREFACE

My intention in this modest-sized book is to discuss the center of the modern ecumenical movement: the unity of the Christian church. Other important and critical parts of the ecumenical movement, such as mission, service to a broken world, and justice—the so-called new church-dividing issues—are mentioned only tangentially in this volume. One should not conclude from this that they are being relegated to insignificance. Ultimately, any division between unity and mission is artificial and unacceptable. The thesis of this volume is that, properly understood, ecumenism is first and foremost a unity issue. "This unity is God's gift in the life of the Church under Christ and the Spirit. Ecumenism is the experience and on-going task of expressing this unity" (*Ecumenism: A Lutheran Commitment,* Preface, An Official Statement of the Lutheran Church in America, adopted by the Eleventh Biennial Convention, September 1982). Only when this is fully appreciated can the other elements be properly understood.

This book seeks to explain this phenomenon to Christians and others, who are often amazed by, and bewildered at, the ecumenical movement—which appears to many to be tearing down old walls of division and developing a view of the visible unity of the church.

Throughout Christianity today there is a consciousness that many historical disagreements between Christians are losing their relevance. Many Christians are at the beginning of a new chapter, where they may achieve a new understanding of the Christian faith liberated from controversies of the past, so that, as a gift from the Spirit of the triune God, the church will be observably more one, holy, catholic, and apostolic.

The pages that follow endeavor to paint, in broad strokes, the alluring picture of all that is happening.

# PREFACE

For the preparation of the manuscript, I am grateful to Katherine Rabenau. Her efforts shortened considerably the time required in making this book ready for publication. Norman Hjelm, the former Director and Senior Editor of Fortress Press, a colleague and friend in many concerns, deserves a special word of thanks for his support of this volume. The idea for this book arose in a conversation with Bishop James R. Crumley, Jr., of the Lutheran Church in America on a long flight during an ecumenical journey. I owe him an expression of gratitude not only for his encouragement of this book but for his commitment to ecumenism: a movement toward church unity.

WILLIAM G. RUSCH

# 1

# THE CHURCH
# AS ONE

Most Christians as they worship recite, at least on occasion, the Nicene (or more accurately, the Nicene-Constantinopolitan) Creed which dates from the year A.D. 381. In this creed they confess, "We believe in one, holy, catholic and apostolic church." This sentence of the creed is the first enunciation in the history of the church of the four characteristic marks or notes of the church. A complete understanding of Christian teaching about the church would require attention to all four of these characteristics. Such an understanding is beyond the purpose and limits of this volume, which will limit itself to the first mark: "one," or unity.

It is obvious both to Christians and to those who do not accept the claims of Christianity that, while Christians may affirm that the church is one, present realities and the sweep of the history of the church painfully disclose that Christians are divided. In spite of the fact that Christians may state their belief in one church, they have lived and worshiped not merely in isolation from one another but in serious disagreement and even hatred. Those who insisted on the name of Christian found they could not gather around the same altar to partake of the sacraments or hear together the proclaimed Word. Clearly they were not able to reflect the statement of their own faith— one church.

This contradiction has caused Christians in every time to be troubled about the scandal of their divisions. In our own day the Swiss theologian Karl Barth has written:

There is no doubt that to the extent that Christendom does consist of actually different and opposing *Churches,* to that extent it denies practically what it confesses theoretically—the unity and the singularity of

1

God, of Jesus Christ, of the Holy Spirit. There may be good grounds for the rise of these divisions. There may be serious obstacles to their removal. There may be many things which can be said by way of interpretation and mitigation. But this does not alter the fact that every division as such is a deep riddle, a *scandal.*[1]

Such views had already early in this century caused committed Christians of different denominational labels and from every continent to take up the task and the opportunity to remove this scandal. These efforts, collectively known as the ecumenical movement, have as their primary goal the experiencing as a gift from God the visible unity of the church. The phrase "visible unity" has been taken up by the ecumenical movement to emphasize that although the community of faith in its allegiance to its one Lord is indeed always one, this oneness must find visible expression among its members. In the next chapter the history of the ecumenical movement will be outlined. Here something of its rationale will be explored.

In its quest the ecumenical movement can prompt a number of questions. Why should Christians be concerned with the oneness of the church as a visible unity? Is it merely a matter of effectiveness, efficiency, or even public image? This inquiry leads to other issues. What is meant by "the unity of the church"? Is unity only uniformity? How is division to be understood? Are all differences among Christians wrong? Is division the same thing as diversity? Answers to such questions can begin to be found by looking again at that statement from the creed: "We believe in one, holy, catholic and apostolic church." In using these marks of the church, the creed witnesses to what Scripture itself says about the community of faith which is described in the New Testament as the church.

The biblical message of the unity of the community of faith is found not simply in the New Testament but also in the Hebrew Scriptures. The first Christians were indeed aware that the New Testament church was not something completely new but had antecedents in the Old Testament. The word "people" occurs over fifteen hundred times in the Hebrew Scriptures. The term "people of God" becomes a technical phrase for Israel as the chosen people of God. A dominant theme in the Old Testament is the description of a people, both diverse and united, who are to be God's instrument to witness to the nations.

This can be observed as early as Genesis 12. At the beginning of sacred history Abraham is called. This call of God includes the promise to make Abraham a great people and through him to bless all the nations of the earth. The descendants of Abraham will be unique, but all the nations will refer to Abraham as the father of that people. Here, then, is the unity of a people who will descend from Abraham. There is also a recognition of all the nations of the earth in their diversity who will be united in him whom God has called.

The combination of unity and diversity continues in the narratives about the twelve patriarchs who descend from Abraham, Isaac, and Jacob. A design emerges as these patriarchs provide the origin of the tribes (Genesis 49). The twelve tribes of the one people become a characteristic structure that God furnishes to his plan of salvation in both covenants. The unity and diversity of the twelve continues in the New Testament with the twelve disciples. In the Old Testament the twelve tribes of Israel express a perfect unity of people and an equal election of twelve tribes which form this people chosen by God. The organization signifies both the gathering into unity of one people and a diversity in that each tribe has its own existence which continues.

After the reign of King Solomon and the division of the people into two kingdoms the same dialectic can be observed (1 Kings 12). The Northern Kingdom and that of Judah formed one people of God. A division had been allowed by God, but there was a center of communion at Jerusalem to which Israel and Judah equally had to address themselves. There were two realms, but the allegiance, belonging to a people gathered in one worship, keeps the unity willed by God and recalled by the prophets.

It is the prophets who seek to recall God's chosen and unfaithful people back to their vocation of unity. The tragedy of a people who broke their covenants with God is the context for the prophets' work. Second Isaiah (Isaiah 60) strives to restore the scattered unity of Israel so that it may be a light to the nations and God's salvation may extend throughout the world. The messages of Ezekiel (Ezek. 20:34; 34:12–13) and Hosea (Hosea 14) were similar. God brings judgment on his faithless people but also offers his promise of reconciliation.

3

Now the notion of a remnant becomes prominent. This small group of united faithful will become witnesses of God's love for all the nations.

The message of the Old Testament accounts of the people of Israel is clear. God creates a united and diverse people to be his witness to the nations. Even in the face of repetitious sin God intends by means of this diverse one people to reveal his love for humankind. In the course of this story of several centuries there is a conspicuous lack of uniformity within this one people, and even full agreement is rare. Unanimity among the people probably exists only at the departure from Egypt, the crossing of the Red Sea, and the covenant event at Sinai, and even at such times it is short-lived. The unity of the people is not a uniformity among the people; rather, it reveals itself as a unity in worship of this diverse people as they gather as a single people in the worship of the one God.

The New Testament documents disclose both a continuity with the Old Testament presentation and a discontinuity of further developments and changes. All of the New Testament statements about the church reflect specific historical situations. The New Testament does not give one timeless picture of the church; rather, it presents a number of ecclesiological types (impressions). The Gospels portray a Jesus who made fellowship a reality among those who followed him. Nevertheless Jesus did not, according to the Gospel accounts, organize any clearly defined communities. The immediate post-Easter community was greatly influenced by Old Testament salvation history and apocalyptic expectations of the reestablishment of the people of the twelve tribes. A decisive step is taken by those called Hellenists (Acts 7 and 8), for with them Christianity begins to move out beyond the Jewish people and disengage itself from Jewish religion. This is seen in the Book of Acts and the various letters where Gentiles became disciples without first becoming Jewish proselytes (Acts 15). With this development it is no longer accurate to speak of a renewed people of God; one must speak now of a new people in contrast to the old.

The New Testament offers the picture of an incessant process of change not only in ecclesiology but in eschatology, soteriology, and anthropology. The rule of Christ under the Spirit is the source of unity, but it is a unity that presupposes diversity. It is never a uniformity that leads to sterility and loss of all common life. In the New Testament, life and fellowship in the Holy Spirit express themselves as a unity held together by tensions. Again there is unity and diversity. The tensions and differences between Jewish Christian and Gentile Christian churches, between Paul and the enthusiasts at Corinth, between John and emerging catholicism were considerable. Despite all its vicissitudes, tensions, and contradictions, early Christianity proclaimed one church. This can be seen in the different theologies preserved in the New Testament.

For the apostle Paul, unity is at the center of his thought and theology. This is because he associates so closely the unity of the church with his Christology. In Paul's pastoral work and thinking about the church, concern for its unity is obvious. He employs images such as "the people of God," "the temple of God," and "the body of Christ," and in connection with discussions of baptism and the Lord's Supper (1 Cor. 10:17; 12:12 seq.). As there is one Christ for all, Jew and Gentile, so there is one gospel of salvation for sinners (Gal. 1:6–9). If the Word from the cross which offers justification to sinners is not held fast as the only ground of salvation, then the unity of the church is lost. Paul defends the unity of the church in his conflicts with Gnostic groups and Judaizers by means of his teachings about Christology and soteriology. Also he sees that when the unity of the church is threatened by various groups in Corinth or by Peter's conduct in Antioch, Christology and soteriology are also in danger (Gal. 2:11–21).

On the other hand, Paul recognized much diversity that did not cause concern for the unity of the church. Different organizational patterns of Christian communities in the New Testament did not call their unity into question. Even in the area of Christology uniformity was not required. Many details of Christology of the church of Jerusalem diverged from Paul's thinking but did not affect the unity he shared with this church (Gal. 2:1–10). Paul must have known that the original Jewish Christian community used titles such as "Messiah," "Son of Man," "Son of David," and "Servant of God" as key christological expressions. Nevertheless, as the Hellenistic communities, Paul had a preference for terms such as *kyrios* and "Son of God" to articulate his Christology. In recognizing this diversity, Paul still insisted that the church must be one if it does not want to lose its qualification as the church of God. His care for the collection for the Jerusalem community indicates that it is a matter of the unity of all Christianity and not just the communities that he established (1 Corinthians 16; Gal. 2:10).

In the Gospels the unity of the church is also presented. The Gospel of Mark, which does not use the word "ecclesia," issues a warning before the appearances of false Christs and prophets at the end of time (Mark 13:22). This warning reveals that a time will come when the true community of the elect will be clearly recognized. This would be the case so that no false Christ could seduce Christians.

As the church began to extend throughout the known world, it became important to ensure that it refer back in an unmistakable manner to Jesus of Nazareth. Thus the motive of unity is present in the Gospel of Matthew although in a less obvious form. The founding of the church on Peter and the delivery of the power of the keys to him and to the other disciples imply a threat to the unity of the church, which in the understanding of this Gospel is the true people of God in place of Israel (Matt. 16:18 seq.; 18:18). The parable of the meal (Matt. 22:2–14) is evidence of a Matthean ecclesiology, representing the church as a body of elect and nonelect whose unity is constantly in danger.

Both the Gospel of Luke and the Book of Acts are strongly influenced by attention to the unity of the church. The so-called council of apostles (Acts 15) takes up, in the discussion about the relationship of Jewish law and the Gentile Christian community, the unity of the church composed of Jews and Gentiles. Unity is addressed in Peter's argumentation (Acts 15:9–11) and in the reply of James (Acts 15:13–18) using the image of David's dwelling. The quality of the unity is given as the unity of a community of God, his new people, made up of Jews and Gentiles. This unity is strongly presented in the Book of Acts in the farewell speech of Paul to the leaders of the community from Ephesus. This address foretells that the time of peace in the first community will soon end. The idyllic situation of correct belief, common ownership, unity of heart and soul, recognized authority of the apostles, and a common ordering of the church (Acts 2:42 seq.; 4:32 seq.; 5:12 seq.; 9:31; 15; 20:17) will not continue after Paul's departure when individuals will arise within the community and draw away the disciples (Acts 20:29 seq.). Paul urges his audience to watchfulness to preserve the unity of the church which is endangered by the end of the original period of peace. The Book of Acts comes from a time of crisis when the communities of Asia Minor that were founded by Paul have largely been destroyed by Gnostic teaching. The intention of Acts is to absolve Paul of the responsibility of this catastrophe. It is also to encourage church leaders of its day to work at the restoration of the unity of the church with the same zeal as Paul himself.

The Johannine literature is also much interested in questions of unity. The departure prayer of Jesus (John 17) is a request for the unity of the church (John 17:11, 20–23). This Gospel, as no other, has Jesus speak directly and clearly of his concern for the unity of the community, a unity which it experiences in unity with God. According to Johannine theology, this unity cannot be established by institutions or dogma and be made visible. It is present only through the Word of proclamation in which Jesus is present in his unity with the Father. There is no disadvantage, because the unity of believers is dependent on belief in Jesus. Here the Fourth Gospel's understanding of succession is involved. Unity with Christ leads to a unity of believers, and in the unity of the disciples is reproduced the unity of believers with the Father and the Son.

Generally it can be concluded from the New Testament witness that the unity of the community, either as a fact or a claim, becomes an issue when false Christian teaching is present. Yet this does not mean that in the New Testament unity is to be seen only as orthodoxy. The understanding of unity as a unity of teaching is first expressed in the middle of the second century in the writings of the church father Irenaeus. The diversity of teaching acknowledged by Paul was not viewed in the New Testament as a detriment to unity. This, however, should not lead to the conclusion that the unity of the church was viewed as completely independent from teaching or a confessional stance and only a matter for the eschatology of the church. The divisions in the community of Corinth not only were an offense against the celebration of the Eucharist but resulted from a false teaching, a false proclamation that distorted the cross of Christ.

7

In the New Testament a diversity of concepts of teachings per se should not be understood as an obstacle to the unity of the church. This is because the place of unity is in the person of Jesus Christ, whose word and work mean the salvation of the world. Still the discussion about the teaching of error in the Pastorals and 2 Peter is significant and quite different from what is found in Paul. In place of argumentative confrontation there is a demand of appeal for distance from errors of teaching (1 Tim. 6:20) or the rejection of enemies suspected of immorality (2 Peter 2). The unity of the church is kept because no one wants to live in a fellowship with errors of teaching, perceived in a difference of teaching. When differences of teaching result in church division, then there is presupposed an authoritative understanding of teaching. The high regard for unity is evident with different substantiation in the deutero-Pauline writings, the Catholic letters, and Hebrews. The unity of the church continues to be understood in the New Testament even when it is not expressly mentioned. This unity is explained with various rationales. The New Testament reflects an instructive diversity and unity. If Christology and soteriology are sound at their core, this diversity is seen as an enrichment of the unity.

Nevertheless, with its considerable diversity the New Testament has a remarkable unanimity on many aspects of unity. Church unity is not a desirable feature of life in the church, it is a condition of the church's existence. The unity of the church derives from its one Lord. The one Christ is present in every local community. The church is not understood as an invisible entity. It is not a Platonic idea; the church has an actual bodily existence. The local congregations are not a federation of a larger whole. They are united by a common participation in the one Christ. Locality and universality are not seen in contradiction. The church as a body may have many organs, but the New Testament knows only one body in which there is no place for sect or sectarianism. The New Testament does not know of denominations or churches (in the sense of different and opposing confessions). It recognizes diversity but not divisions. Paul insisted to the Corinthians that there be no divisions in the body of Christ (1 Cor. 1:10; 12:25), and church parties he reckoned as one of the works of the flesh (Gal. 5:20). A survey of the biblical literature yields only one conclusion: one church with a richness of diversity in theology, worship forms, and structures that knows tensions and disputes; but divisions and large numbers of Christians separated from full fellowship with one another are not to be found.

This unity and diversity of the church affirmed in Scripture was largely maintained in the Western church for centuries despite controversy and theological disputes. Long-lasting divisions had occurred in the Eastern church after the Council of Chalcedon in 451, and the churches of the West and the East experienced a rupture often assigned too precisely to the year 1054. Actually a more accurate date may be 1204. In spite of these conditions nothing like modern denominationalism had developed. This had to await the sixteenth century. By this time many misunderstandings of the faith and abuses of practice had arisen within the Western church. Earlier attempts to correct this situation had met with little success. Martin Luther and other reformers sought to call the church of their day to an evangelical reform. Their intention was neither to divide the Western church nor to establish a new church. Whenever the charge was made that Luther and his followers were departing from the church, they reacted strongly, declaring that they were part of the one universal church. Contrary to their intention, their efforts at reform resulted in divisions in the church of the West. In the course of the heated events of this time, the Lutheran Reformers set forth their views in a number of writings. By 1580 several of these documents had been collected into *The Book of Concord.* The texts assembled in this volume assumed a special importance for Lutherans and explained clearly what the Lutheran Reformation taught, including what it held about the unity of the church.

*The Book of Concord* contains three documents that did not come from the disputes of the sixteenth century: the Apostles' Creed, the Nicene Creed, and the Athanasian Creed. The primary Reformation document of the collection is the unaltered Augsburg Confession of 1530. This text, written by Philipp Melanchthon, was presented to the Diet of Augsburg in 1530. Representing the theological consensus of those who accepted the Lutheran Reformation, it became the most authoritative confession for Lutherans. *The Book of Concord* also included the Apology of the Augsburg Confession, written by Melanchthon to elucidate the teaching of the Confession over against the misunderstandings of its opponents; the Smalcald Articles of 1537, from the pen of Luther, which were intended for an anticipated general council; the Treatise on the Power and Primacy of the Pope, by Melanchthon, which completes themes raised in the Augsburg Confession; Luther's Large and Small Catechisms as summary presentations of Reformation doctrine for the laity; and the Formula of Concord of 1577 in a short and a long form, which resolved doctrinal disputes over the interpretation of the Augsburg Confession.

All of these documents of *The Book of Concord* were generally regarded as confessions by the churches of the Lutheran Reformation, that is, these churches assumed a responsibility for them. They were no longer considered merely the writings of individuals. On the contrary, the claim was made not that Lutheran churches are speaking here but that the one, holy, catholic and apostolic church can find its teaching in these confessions. These documents are "confessions" because they are seen as primary expositions of Scripture, witness to the gospel itself, expounded by the church itself. Thus as confessions they make the claim to be the obligatory model of all of the church's preaching and teaching without limit of time or space. Edmund Schlink has pointed out that they call for a cognizance of their claim as the church's normative exposition of Scripture and for a definite stand with respect to that claim.[2] As Lutherans have tested these claims they have developed principles of interpretation. A prevailing view among many is that greater weight be given to the Augsburg Confession and Luther's Small Catechism than to the other documents. Some Lutheran churches have refused to recognize the Formula of Concord as a confession and see it as the beginning of post-Reformation developments.

Among the many threads that run through *The Book of Concord* one of the most prominent is the insistence that the teaching of the Reformers is not conceived as the dogma of a new church but as the correct teaching of the one, holy, catholic and apostolic church. It can be seen in the inclusion of the three ecumenical creeds of the early church and in the numerous citations of church fathers, both Eastern and Western. The conclusion of the Augsburg Confession states:

It must not be thought that anything has been said or introduced out of hatred or for the purpose of injuring anybody, but we have related only matters of which we have considered it necessary to adduce and mention in order that they may be made very clear that we have introduced nothing, either in doctrine or in ceremonies, that is contrary to Holy Scripture or the universal Christian Church.[3]

The Formula of Concord likewise declares:

Since in ancient times the true Christian doctrine as it was correctly and soundly understood was drawn together out of God's Word in brief articles or chapters against the aberrations of heretics, we further pledge allegiance to the three general Creeds, the Apostles', the Nicene and the Athanasian, as glorious confessions of the faith succinct, Christian, and based upon the Word of God.[4]

The intention of the Lutheran Confessions, and especially the Augsburg Confession, was to establish a basis for unity rather than division. The Preface to the Augsburg Confession discloses that the confessors believed that Christians

could unite ... in agreement on one Christian truth ... put aside whatever may not have been rightly interpreted or treated by either side, to have all of us embrace and adhere to a single, true religion and live together in unity and in one fellowship and church, even as we are all enlisted under one Christ.[5]

They were asking at Augsburg for a unity in diversity as revealed in Scripture itself. They remained committed to this ideal of unity with no interest in schism, although the course of history led in another direction. In other words, the original purpose of the Lutheran Confessions was to be a bridge to join together various theological parties within one church. They intended to identify the common center of the faith, describe what agreement was required for unity, and indicate those areas where differences should not affect unity.

The key teaching of the Lutheran Confessions is justification by grace through faith. This is the criterion for judging all church doctrine and life. It is not one doctrine among several. Not accidentally, the Augsburg Confession places the article on justification (Article 4) immediately after the articles on the teaching of the early church and before the articles on the ministry and the church. Here is taught that

God's justification of the sinner in Jesus Christ is really given to a person through the Holy Spirit (see Augsburg Confession, Articles 4, 5, 13). The gospel is nothing else than the promise that God receives into communion sinners who have faith for Christ's sake and through that faith makes them his own. The gospel is the event that occurs in proclamation and in the administration of the sacraments. The proclamation and administration are judged as to whether they serve the gospel or obscure or deny it. So too in teaching about the church, the Confessions see the center of the Reformation, the gospel, the doctrine of justification, at issue. The Confessions link the question of unity of the church to the principle article of faith—justification by grace through faith apart from works. In fact, they see it as the only standard for true unity.

This is exhibited most clearly in Article 7 of the Augsburg Confession. Succinct and simple, it reads:

> It is also taught among us that one holy Christian Church will be and remain forever. This is the assembly of all believers among whom the Gospel is preached in its purity and the holy sacraments are administered according to the Gospel. For it is sufficient for the true unity of the Christian church that the Gospel be preached in conformity with the pure understanding of it and the sacraments be administered in accordance with the divine Word. It is not necessary for the true unity of the Christian church that ceremonies instituted by men should be observed uniformly in all places. It is as Paul says in Ephesians 4:4–5, "There is one body and one Spirit, just as you were called to one hope that belongs to your call, one Lord, one faith, one baptism."[6]

The article teaches that what is essential for both the existence and the unity of the church is that the gospel be preached in its pure form and the sacraments be administered in accord with it. Where both of these things happen, there is the church. Where Christians and churches concur on this, there is the unity of the church, and all that is needed for church fellowship has been met. The article anchors the existence and the unity of the church in true proclamation of the gospel in Word and Sacrament. The marks of the church here are Word and Sacrament. Gospel is meant as the proclamation of forgiveness, not as the possession of doctrine, not as the depository of doctrinal propositions. Likewise, the article does not speak about knowledge of the sacraments but about their administration according to the gospel. The church is characterized not by the possession of doctrine about the sacraments but by their actual giving and receiving. Thus in that assembly where the gospel Word is preached, "in conformity with pure understanding of it," agreement occurs. When the creeds of the ancient church and the sacraments are practiced in accord with this gospel Word, there is the church.

Article 7 also draws a sharp distinction between what is absolutely necessary and what are areas of responsible freedom. It clearly states that uniformity in rites and ceremonies is not required. These words should not be taken too strictly. They include everything pertaining to order in the church that has been established in the liberty of faith. Uniformity of order in the church can be an asset, but such uniformity is not required for unity. Unity of creed is of incomparably greater importance than uniformity of external ordinances. The unity of the church cannot exist without it. Yet the unity of the church can exist where this unity has only partially or not yet been articulated in credal statements. Organization of the church is not an insignificant concern, but the church does not need a definite form or organization to be the church or to be united. Church discipline is important; the church is to practice it. Such discipline is not a mark of the church. Works of love should be performed by those in the church, but such works do not constitute the church or make its unity. The Lutheran Confessions are clear: the *preaching* of the gospel and the *administration* of the sacraments are the norms for the church and unity between churches. Therefore they distinguish between what is needed for unity and areas of genuine Christian freedom—a unity and a diversity.[7]

The original irenic intention of the Lutheran Confessions did not prevail either with Roman Catholics or with other reformers. By the seventeenth century hard lines of division had been set in the Western church. Unity in diversity was replaced by competing divisions. Modern denominationalism was born in Europe and promptly exported to the New World. In all of these events the primary function of the Lutheran Confessions to be a bridge preserving unity between Christians of legitimate diversity was lost. Either they became a barrier to unity—not only between Lutherans and other Christians but between Lutherans and other Lutherans—or they were largely ignored. Theodore G. Tappert described four sharply divergent attitudes toward the Confessions in nineteenth-century American Lutheranism.[8] They are (1) rejection as obsolete documents of only historical value, (2) revision of the documents to update them, (3) unconditional subscription to *The Book of Concord,* with no distinction between fundamental and nonfundamental articles, and (4) historical and practical interpretation rather than dogmatic. All of these positions in varying degrees represent a departure from the original function of the Confessions. When the Augsburg Confession and other confessions did receive attention in the last century they often occupied a central role amid bitter clashes of Lutheran groups. Many Lutherans in America followed a repristination of the teachings of Lutheran Orthodoxy of the seventeenth century. Underlying this outlook was the presupposition that purity and unity of doctrine are foremost. Pure Lutheran doctrine was viewed as a homogeneous whole. Later confessions only clarify what was enunciated in the Augsburg Confession. The Lutheran system becomes permanently fixed and irreformable because it agrees perfectly with the changeless divine Word. It follows that there is nothing in the realm of doctrine left to explore among Christians. Some Lutherans drew this conclusion; others attempted to guarantee orthodox doctrinal unity but to be somewhat more flexible in church practice. The nineteenth century was not a happy time for relationships between Lutherans and other Christians or among Lutherans. Part of the reason for this was the view that the Lutheran Confessions identified a denomination in distinction from other groups that may in varying degrees be seen as church. Rather than functioning as a bridge, the Confessions became the constitution of a denomination and a barrier to other Christians.

In this century great changes have taken place in the relationships among American Lutherans, and between Lutherans and other Christians. This has occurred in large measure because of a shift in interpretation of the Confessions by many Lutherans. This new situation can be seen in the position of the General Synod in 1913 affirming the unaltered Augsburg Confession as a correct exhibition of the faith and doctrine of the church and recognizing other symbols as expositions of Lutheran doctrine of great historical and interpretive value.

The United Lutheran Church in America announced in its Washington Declaration in 1920 a comprehensive statement on the church and its external relationships which stressed in a positive way the catholicity of the church and the need for proper cooperation between churches.[9] To many these events were occasioned by a recovery of an understanding of the original intention of the Lutheran Confessions. *The Theology of the Lutheran Confessions,* by Edmund Schlink,[10] written in German in 1940, appeared in English in 1961 and was influential in this recovery. Robert W. Jenson, in a paper written for the first series of Lutheran-Episcopal dialogue in the United States in 1972, entitled "Lutheran Conditions for Communion in Holy Things," documented the ecumenical potential in a hermeneutic of the Confessions that saw them as ecumenical resources for greater unity.[11] In 1974 the Lutheran Church in America rewrote its "Evangelical and Representational Principles" to emphasize with whom the church should cooperate rather than with whom it may not cooperate. The celebration of the 450th anniversary of the Augsburg Confession in 1980, with the attendant question of possible Roman Catholic recognition of this confessional document, accelerated an understanding of at least this Lutheran Confession as a basis for unity. Considerable literature was produced.[12]

The recovery of the intention of the Confessions of the sixteenth century includes a recognition that it is not possible to repristinate sixteenth-century conditions. The context of the Augsburg Confession no longer exists today. The practice of fellowship and visible unity, while in extreme danger in 1530, had not yet been lost. The present challenge is not to maintain visible unity but to attempt to regain it. Thus the Confessions cannot be merely applied to today. They must be interpreted. The Confessions must be reread in their historical context, in the light of modern biblical study, and through living encounters with representatives of other confessional traditions. When this is done, the ecumenical potential of *The Book of Concord* is realized once again. It offers a commitment to church unity in tension with appropriate diversity. This has allowed Lutherans, while not surrendering the goal of the formulation of a theological consensus of confession, to recognize multiple expressions of doctrine, life, and action as valid expressions of the gospel and thus fulfilling the requirements of Article 7 of the Augsburg Confession. Lutherans still place considerable importance on a common formulation and expression of theological consensus of confession, but many are now willing to acknowledge that the traditional principle of doctrinal conversation and agreement first, and only then church fellowship, is too rigidly one-sided and without the support of the Augsburg Confession. There has come about an awareness of an interrelation between the fact of living and experiencing fellowship and agreement on faith and doctrine.

This interpretation of the confessional position, while seen by some as a recent development, is claimed by its proponents as a more faithful view of the intentions of the Lutheran Reformers. It found official approval by the Lutheran Church in America in its official statement, *Ecumenism: A Lutheran Commitment,* which declares:

> Yet Article VII of the Augsburg Confession continues to be ecumenically liberating because of its insistence that agreement in the Gospel suffices for Christian unity. This interpretation of Article VII frees Lutherans as they seek to promote the proclamation of the message of God's saving action in Jesus Christ, to enter into church fellowship without insisting on doctrinal or ecclesiastical uniformity. Lutherans still place considerable emphasis on common formulation and expression of theological consensus. Yet they recognize from this article that, where there is consensus on the Gospel, there is room for a living and experiencing of fellowship within the context of seeking larger theological agreement.[13]

In the course of this chapter the Bible and the Lutheran Confessions have been examined to see what they teach about the unity of the church. Some clear conclusions can be drawn from this examination. The unity of God's church is at the heart of the Christian faith. It is God's will for his people. Christians should be one not because it is expedient or efficient but because their God has called into existence one people. This unity is not seen as a uniformity; it always exists in a tension with a diversity. This diversity is an indication of the richness of the Christian tradition, a potential, not a problem. Unfortunately this diversity turned into division. Denominations came into being because of this division. Yet in the sixteenth century when one of the most serious divisions in the church was occurring, this was not the intention of the Reformers. The Lutheran confessors desired to preserve the unity of the church in a richness of diversity as long as they were able to proclaim the gospel. Unfortunate incidents on both sides of the dispute made a difficult situation impossible. The Western church was split. In subsequent centuries Lutherans ignored the insights of their own confessions as to what was needed to restore visible unity among Christians. In the last seventy years a number of developments have occurred that have made it possible for Lutherans and other Christians to move beyond the divisions of their past to a greater manifestation of the unity they share under Christ. This is the story of the modern ecumenical movement, which will be the subject of the next chapter.

## NOTES

1. Karl Barth, *Church Dogmatics* (Edinburgh: T. & T. Clark, 1957), vol. 4, pt. 1, 675. Italics added.

2. Edmund Schlink, *The Theology of the Lutheran Confessions* (Philadelphia: Fortress Press, 1961), xvii–xxix.

3. The confessions of the Lutheran churches may be found in the original German or Latin in *Die Bekenntnisschriften der evangelisch-lutherischen Kirche* (Göttingen: Vandenhoeck & Ruprecht, 1959). The best English edition is *The Book of Concord,* trans. and ed. by Theodore G. Tappert (Philadelphia: Fortress Press, 1959). The quotation is from the Tappert edition (hereafter Tappert), 95.

4. Tappert, 504.

5. Tappert, 25.

6. Tappert, 32.

7. This interpretation of the Lutheran Confessions and especially of the Augsburg Confession, Article 7, is in harmony with the view held by Schlink, *The Theology of the Lutheran Confessions,* 194–225, and Eric W. Gritsch and Robert W. Jenson, *Lutheranism: The Theological Movement and Its Confessional Writings* (Philadelphia: Fortress Press, 1976), 166–78.

8. Theodore G. Tappert, "The Symbols of the Church," in *What Lutherans Are Thinking,* by E. C. Fendt (Columbus: Wartburg Press, 1947), 343–67.

9. For a detailed description of this history, see E. Clifford Nelson, ed., *The Lutherans in North America* (Philadelphia: Fortress Press, 1975), and E. Theodore Bachmann, *The Ecumenical Involvement of the LCA Predecessor Bodies,* rev. 2d ed. (New York: Division for World Mission and Ecumenism, Lutheran Church in America, 1983).

10. Schlink, *The Theology of the Lutheran Confessions.*

11. Robert W. Jenson, "Lutheran Conditions for Communion in Holy Things," in *Lutheran-Episcopal Dialogue: A Progress Report* (Cincinnati: Forward Movement Publications, 1972), 127–38.

12. Heinrich Fries and others, *Confessio Augustana: Hindernis oder Hilfe* (Regensburg: Verlag Friedrich Pustet, 1979). Joseph A. Burgess, ed., *The Role of the Augsburg Confession: Catholic and Lutheran Views* (Philadelphia: Fortress Press, 1980). George W. Forell and James F. McCue, eds., *Confessing One Faith: A Joint Commentary on the Augsburg Confession by Lutheran and Catholic Theologians* (Minneapolis: Augsburg Publishing House, 1982).

13. *Ecumenism: A Lutheran Commitment* (New York: Lutheran Church in America, 1982), 14.

# 2

# A BRIEF HISTORY
# OF THE ECUMENICAL MOVEMENT

In chapter 1 we surveyed the teaching of Scripture and of *The Book of Concord* on the unity of the church, both of which propose the ideal of visible unity in creative tension with diversity. It is a sad observation on history to note that the church has rarely enjoyed this unity, but more often than not has been involved *not* in unity with diversity but in division. This chapter will describe how some of these divisions occurred and how committed individuals and churches, especially in the twentieth century, have responded to the promptings of God's Spirit to overcome them.

In the fourth century one of the first major divisions in the church arose over the relationship between God the Father and the Word of God, his Son. This controversy about the doctrine of the Trinity began in the year 318 as a result of the teaching of Arius, a priest at Alexandria in Egypt. His name has been given to the teaching known as Arianism, which in its simplest formulation declared that Jesus Christ as the Word is the first of the created order but not God. This doctrine deeply divided the church for years. Many different theological groupings arose. Bishops, emperors, and multitudes of believers were enmeshed in a bitter dispute before agreement on a teaching faithful to the Scriptures and the tradition of the church could be formulated. In 325 the Council of Nicaea approved a creed which taught that Jesus Christ is consubstantial with the Father. This creed was interpreted differently by various groups. Sometimes it was ignored. It was only at the Council of Constantinople in 381 that a vision of the creed of 325 was affirmed as the church's teaching about the Trinity so as to end the dispute. Although the division begun by Arius was gradually resolved, the dispute he started affected the history of the church and Europe.

In the next century, conflicts developed about Christology, the relationship of the incarnated Word to the human Jesus. These issues were complicated by the use of differing philosophical vocabularies and political motivations of many of the key figures. Nestorius the Patriarch of Constantinople seemed to teach a division of the human and the divine in Jesus, so that Christ's unity was lost. The theological school at Alexandria taught that the divinity of Christ absorbed the humanity, so that there was only a single nature in Christ, and thus the word "monophysite" (one nature) entered the debate. If Nestorius appeared to destroy the one person of Christ in two persons, Alexandrian theologians seemed to present a Christ who was not really human. The theological school of Antioch was vulnerable to being charged with the other extreme: it taught a human Christ, who was not really divine. A series of councils were held. Finally, the Council of Ephesus in 431 and the Council of Chalcedon in 451 led to positions accepted throughout most of the church. Ephesus declared that Mary was to be called the Mother of God (Theotokos), a view rejected by Nestorius. Chalcedon affirmed Christ as both true man and true God according to his person. Many Christians of the time refused to acknowledge the formulation of Chalcedon. Separated churches came into being in Egypt (the Coptic church), Syria, Armenia, and much of Mesopotamia. Often called Monophysite or non-Chalcedonian churches because of their repudiation of the Council of Chalcedon and acceptance of Alexandrian theology, they have more recently been described as Oriental churches to contrast them with Orthodox churches which accept the Chalcedonian teaching. Unlike the divisions over the Trinity, the ruptures over Christology have continued to the present day. Eastern Orthodoxy is divided into two groupings depending on whether or not the Council of Chalcedon is affirmed. This division weakened the Eastern church at the time when it had to face the rise of Islam, and deprived the Chalcedonian churches in East and West of the rich Semitic traditions of theological reflection, thus impoverishing theological thought in the Byzantine East and the Roman West.

Another painful division was also developing, this time between the church of Rome and the church of Constantinople. Many factors, theological and nontheological, contributed to this estrangement.

Western theology is more pragmatic, with a focus on questions of salvation and ecclesiology. Eastern theology is contemplative, concerned to elaborate a theology of the Trinity and Christ. Different mentalities led to suspicions and reciprocal condemnations. It became clear that East and West held differing perceptions of the role of the church of Rome and its bishop in the service of the universal church. The insertion of the word *filioque* ("and from the Son") into the Nicene-Constantinopolitan Creed caused sharp theological disputes. The different cultures of the Eastern and Western empires also contributed to the lack of understanding. Thus the churches found themselves gradually divided, unable to celebrate the liturgy together or to share the Eucharist. This state of affairs did not, as some have suggested, arise suddenly in the year 1054 with the excommunication placed on the altar of Hagia Sophia by Cardinal Humbert and the counter-anathemas of Patriarch Michael Cerularius. There is evidence of relations after 1054. Certainly the sack of Constantinople by Crusaders from the West in 1204 was an irreparable event which dashed hopes of reconciliation and contributed to further division. Seventy years later, in 1274, the Council of Lyons was convoked by Pope Gregory X. It endeavored to reestablish unity between the Roman and the Greek churches. It did not achieve this goal. By 1289 the unity proclaimed at Lyons had come to an end. The Council of Florence, which met from 1438 to 1445, had as its chief object reunion of the two churches. The Greeks, under considerable pressure from the Turkish threat, submitted to the Western church on a number of theological points. A decree of union was signed on 5 July 1439, but it proved to be ephemeral and was quickly spurned after Eastern representatives returned to their churches. By the thirteenth century the slowly evolving division between Eastern Orthodoxy and the Latin churches of the West had solidified, and it continued into the twentieth.

Thus the opening of the sixteenth century saw Eastern Christianity split between Orthodox and Oriental churches, and Eastern and Western churches divided. The fabric of the Western church appeared to have remained intact, but this appearance was somewhat deceiving. Several centuries earlier, individual voices already had been raised calling for a reform to correct the abuses and corruptions that were growing in the Church of Rome. Most of this concern went unheeded. In 1517 Martin Luther protested against the corruption of Rome and the sale of indulgences, urging a return to a Christianity without these excesses—a Christianity based on the gospel of justification by faith. Luther did not wish to split the church. It was Rome's intractability that caused the break between the Church of Rome and Luther and his followers. The Confession of Augsburg in 1530 did not, in spite of its intentions, preserve the visible unity of the Western church. The social and political conditions of Luther's day allowed him to prevail where earlier reformers had failed. The Western church was divided. In 1529 at the Diet of Speyer the word "protestant" entered the religious vocabulary as followers of the Reformation "protested" against the decisions of the Catholic majority at the Diet. Soon other reformers such as the Swiss theologian Ulrich Zwingli and the French John Calvin appeared. The reforming party was itself divided into many groups. By 1533 the church in England was split from Rome by the activities of Henry VIII. The Church of England established by Augustine of Canterbury in 596 was no longer in union with the church at Rome. By the end of the sixteenth century Congregationalist churches appeared in England and by the beginning of the next century Baptist churches composed of Anabaptists and Mennonites were evident. Neither Western Christianity nor the map of Europe was ever to be the same again after the series of changes between the fourteenth and the seventeenth century which became known as the Reformation. Modern denominationalism found its origins in these changes. Although the Reformers did not intend to fragment the church of the West, that is exactly what happened. This fragmentation was quickly carried to the New World as western European nations began to colonize North and South America. Here in a new context the denomination as a voluntary association of like-minded persons becomes distinctive.

The later centuries reveal additional splits in the church. In 1666 a section of the Russian Orthodox Church refused to accept the liturgical reforms of Patriarch Nikon. Called Old Believers, they were excommunicated. Their number increased significantly in 1721 when Czar Peter the Great suppressed the patriarchate of Moscow and forced the church to accept sweeping reforms. The Old Believers themselves split into two communities. In 1724 a new schism took place in the Roman Catholic Church. The church of Utrecht with three bishops refused to accept the condemnation of Jansenism and separated from Rome. Around 1780 the Anglican Church was affected with another break. John Wesley made provision at about this time for the continuation as a corporate body of the "Year Conference of People called Methodist," and Methodism as a separate denomination with its own system of religious faith and practice was born. In the nineteenth century new denominations such as the Disciples of Christ were established in the United States. During the same century a number of German and Swiss Catholics refused to accept the dogmas of infallibility and ordinary jurisdiction of the pope as defined by the First Vatican Council and seceded from the Church of Rome.

Even the most sketchy review of the history of the church discloses how prevalent have been the divisions in its life that have separated those who claim a common Lord. Less obvious, but critical, are those who amid the divisions have worked for the unity of the church held forth in Scripture. As the above narrative indicates, at times of dispute, when the unity of the church was at issue, genuine efforts were made to avoid division. A major motivation behind the councils of the early church was to resolve disagreements and restore broken fellowship. Several medieval councils sought to bring agreement between the Western and Eastern churches. During the events of the Reformation, Luther, Calvin, and others endeavored to prevent fragmentation and worked for the greatest expression of Christian unity possible. Thus even as divisions were being created, often simultaneous attempts were made to overcome them. Before the sixteenth century a number of colloquies were held such as those at Worms, Ratisbon, and Poissy, but they had little success, usually being seen as unsatisfying compromises. Nevertheless these meetings show that the ecumenical vision was not entirely lost, though it was usually held by individuals contending with formidable difficulties. For the next several centuries it was such committed persons who preserved the vision of unity which had been largely lost by the churches.

In the seventeenth century, ecumenism was in the hands of individuals such as François de Sales, a Quietist who developed a dialogue with Gerard Wolter von Meulen, the Lutheran Abbot of Loccum. Georg Calixtus introduced the concept of unity based on the agreement of the church in the first five centuries, the *Consensus Quinquesaecularis*. Peter Meiderlin, the minister of the Church of St. Anna in Augsburg, authored the irenical expression, "In essentials, unity; in nonessentials, liberty; in all things, charity." This expression was taken up by the Calvinist Gregor Francke in his writings. Others concerned with unity include the English Benedictine John Barnes, Obadiah Walker from Oxford, the French Benedictine Leandrede Saint Martin, and the Italian Gregorio Panzani. In this century, ecumenism was almost exclusively a question of unity in doctrine, with questions of confession and dogma in the foreground. Those who worked in such areas were often lonely pioneers.

The predominant concern in the eighteenth century shifts to unity in life, in piety and in moral life. William Wake, the archbishop of Canterbury, entered into correspondence with L. E. Dupin and Piers Girarden of the Sorbonne with the view to a union between Anglican and Gallican churches. In rites and ceremonies as well as in matters of faith, Wake wished to distinguish between fundamentals and non-fundamentals. Count Nicolaus Ludwig von Zinzendorf, the ardent missionary of Pietism, was in contact with Cardinal de Noailles personally and through letters, and with many others, to promote the unity of the church. Not indifferent to doctrinal matters, Zinzendorf was mainly concerned with practical and personal matters. He wished to recompose Christian unity on the basis of pietistic communities spread throughout the churches as leaven. The last half of the eighteenth century witnessed the preaching of revival. This revival movement, the evangelical awakening, stressed personal conversion and missionary enthusiasm and was to influence thoughts about unity in the nineteenth century.

In 1805 the Baptist missionary William Carey proposed the calling of a missionary conference of all denominations to meet in Capetown, South Africa, in 1810. He hoped such conferences would meet every ten years to discuss missionary problems common to all Christians. Missionary enterprise that promoted contact and understanding between churches resulted in the founding of the British and Foreign Bible Society in 1804. This agency brought Protestants, Roman Catholics, and Orthodox together in its work. C. F. A. Steinkof, who was the first Secretary of the German Christian Fellowship at Basel, developed numerous contacts in the churches. Collaboration seemed possible between Protestant missionary societies and the Eastern churches, with the hope of evangelizing non-Christians. The early years of the nineteenth century were a time of rapprochement between the churches that is little known today. In 1846 the Evangelical Alliance was formed when some eight hundred Christian leaders, mainly from North America and Europe, gathered in London. Fifty-two different churches were represented among the delegates. The Alliance was the only ecumenical organization that arose out of the evangelical revival of the nineteenth century. It stimulated united prayer, held international conferences, and encouraged international Christian education. In 1844 and 1854 respectively, the Young Men's Christian Association and the Young Women's Christian Association were founded. These two organizations, along with the Student Christian Movement, founded by John R. Mott in 1895, provided places where the future leaders of the ecumenical movement would get to know one another, although before 1910 these groups showed little interest in ecumenical questions. These were the years when in the United States such persons as Thomas and Alexander Campbell of the Disciples, Lutheran Samuel Schmucker, Episcopalian William Reed Huntington, and later, Congregationalist Elias B. Sanford laid the groundwork of much ecumenical thinking. Also in the nineteenth century a number of world denominational fellowships were founded. These included the Lambeth Conference of the Anglican communion, which first met in 1867, the Alliance of Reformed Churches Throughout the World Holding the Presbyterian System in 1875, the Methodist Ecumenical Conference in 1881, the Conference of Old Catholic Bishops in 1889, the International Congregational Council in 1891, and the Baptist World Congress in 1905. Also in 1905 the Federal Council was formed in the United States. The denominations themselves sent representatives to the Federal Council of Churches of Christ in America, which as its constitution declared, was to express the fellowship and catholic unity of the church, unite Christian bodies in service for Christ and the world, and encourage devotional fellowship and mutual counsel.[1]

As the twentieth century dawned it seemed that a number of signs were present indicating that the isolation and the sectarianism of the churches were coming to an end. Still, few at the beginning of this century could have guessed the ecumenical advances that would be made in the next eighty years. The slow, uneven progress since the divisions of the church was to accelerate sharply.

The early twentieth century has often been described as the moment of birth of the ecumenical movement. There is indeed much truth in this observation, but as has already been noted, the conditions to make such a birth possible had been developing during the preceding century. Nevertheless, soon after the turn of the century a number of events occurred that launched the modern ecumenical movement. Individually many of these developments were of limited significance; together they can only be seen as a quantum leap forward on the way to greater expressions of Christian unity.

In 1902 Joachim III, patriarch of Constantinople, and the Holy Synod sent an encyclical to all Orthodox churches dealing with the means of possible rapprochement with those who believed in the true God of the Trinity so that the day of union of all Christians might eventually come. The patriarch had in mind two plans: (1) a union of Orthodox churches and (2) programs to enter into contact with non-Orthodox churches.

Six years later, in 1908, Spencer Jones, an Anglican clergyman, and Paul Wattson, a priest of the Episcopal Church in the United States who later became a Roman Catholic, proposed a week of prayer for unity. Under the influence of Abbé Paul Couturier in the 1930s the Week of Prayer was expanded in such a way that Protestants, Orthodox, and Roman Catholics could unite on the basis that "our Lord would grant His Church on earth that peace and unity which were on His mind and purpose, when, on the eve of His Passion, He prayed that all might be one."

From 13 to 23 June 1910, the World Missionary Conference met in Edinburgh. This conference summed up and brought into focus much of the nineteenth century's movement for uniting Christians to give the gospel to the world. Two key figures at Edinburgh were John R. Mott, a Methodist layman and a prodigious worker for Christian unity, and Joseph H. Oldham, a Scot who had studied in Edinburgh, Oxford,

26

and Halle. Mott and Oldham came out of the Student Christian Movement. They were committed to world mission and played an increasing role in the sharing of the ecumenical movement. The Edinburgh Conference was a consultative assembly. It was overwhelmingly Anglo-American. While sometimes its influence has been overdrawn, it did mark a new sense of fellowship among Christians, trained future leaders of the ecumenical movement, and contributed to the calling some seventeen years later of the first conference on Faith and Order. Already at Edinburgh individuals such as Bishop Charles H. Brent saw that Christian unity required an examination of the causes of division and not just discussion of practical cooperation. Before its adjournment the conference took the momentous step of creating a continuation committee. The formation of this committee developed a precedent for the organization later of the ecumenical movement. Many major ecumenical gatherings by the appointment of such continuation committees ensured that their work was carried forward, and the momentum of their results was not lost.

Another important step was the conference of Christian students convened by John R. Mott in 1911 in Constantinople. Representatives of the Eastern churches were invited. This gathering demonstrated that the ecumenical movement was not exclusively Western and Protestant. Associations were formed with Eastern Christians that would have critical effects on future ecumenical relations.

In 1920 the Church of Constantinople issued an encylical to all the churches of the world. It was an invitation to all Christian churches to form a league of churches. Thus the Church of Constantinople became the first church to call for a permanent organ of fellowship and cooperation between the churches. The encyclical had several notable features. It was specifically ecclesiastical; its scope was wide. It recognized both the new opportunities and the dangers of the time. Although the document did not receive wide circulation at the time, historians of the ecumenical movement have noted its significance.[2]

The following year Mott and Oldham presided at a meeting of the International Missionary Council, which was an outgrowth of the Edinburgh Conference. The meeting sought to promote study, coordination, and organization for Christian mission. It elected Mott chairman, established offices in London, and undertook the publication of an international review of mission. Mott's personal contacts with the Orthodox helped make possible a meeting of the Council in 1928 in Jerusalem.

During these same years Archbishop Nathan Söderblom of Uppsala was active in bringing together the churches of the nations involved in World War I to render witness to their common Lord. Söderblom believed an evangelical catholicity was needed to strengthen spiritual unity. A planning meeting in Geneva in 1920 began the preparation for a World Conference on Life and Work in Stockholm in 1925. This conference of more than six hundred was the achievement of Söderblom. It marked a step on the ecumenical road. Most delegates were appointed by their churches. Orthodoxy was strongly represented. An awareness of Christian fellowship, transcending denominational oppositions and national antagonisms, was present. The responsibility of the churches for the whole life of human beings was recognized. The impact of the Stockholm meeting was considerable. A continuation committee was created. The work of Life and Work continued and an important World Conference was held in Oxford in 1937. As a movement along with Faith and Order, it became one of the principal contributors to the formation of a permanent council.

Another major development contemporary with the activities of the International Missionary Council and of Life and Work was the Faith and Order Movement. It had been acknowledged at Edinburgh that true unity between the churches would require doctrinal agreement on the faith and the ordering of the church. While Bishop Charles Brent conceived the idea of a World Conference on Faith and Order, it was Robert Gardiner, an influential Episcopal layman, who became the leader of the enterprise. Planning moved slowly. World War I intervened. Meetings in Geneva in 1920 and in Stockholm in 1925 resulted in the call for a world conference on Faith and Order in 1927 in Lausanne. This gathering brought together 394 persons from 108 churches. The Faith and Order Movement achieved a status and adopted a goal. The Lausanne Conference adopted a statement, "The Call to Unity," and accepted the report, "The Church's Message to the World—The Gospel." Reports on the nature of the church, on a common confession of faith, on ministry, and on sacraments were received. A continuation committee was appointed. The second World Conference of Faith and Order met in Edinburgh in 1937. Its report was fuller and richer than the Lausanne Report. It reflected the advance that had been made in Faith and Order in the ten-year period.

Between 1921 and 1926 another important ecumenical contact took place. At the instigation of Lord Halifax, an Anglican layman, and a French priest, Fernand Portal, a series of conversations were organized, called the Malines Conversations. Five talks took place to see whether Anglican–Roman Catholic relations could be improved. Although the Malines Conversations accomplished little, it would be inaccurate to label them a failure. They set a model that would be taken up and developed years later in official bilateral conversations.

As a result of all this ecumenical activity attempts began to be made for greater coordination. Little happened between 1928 and 1932, but by 1933 it became clear that Faith and Order and Life and Work would achieve greater coordination, which would prepare for the World Council of Churches. Key meetings were held in Princeton in 1935 and at Westfield College in London in 1937. Plans for the integration of Life and Work and Faith and Order into a World Council were discussed both in Edinburgh and Oxford in the same year. Approval was forthcoming, and a conference met at Utrecht in 1938 to draw up a constitution for the World Council. During this process of formation the Federal Council of Churches of Christ in America gave considerable support to the World Council. World War II delayed the creation of the World Council until 1948. But a small staff was in place in Geneva, and the time of war proved to be a time of deepening and intensifying ecumenical fellowship.

Plans began soon after the end of the war to organize a constituting assembly for the World Council of Churches. Some 351 delegates from 147 churches gathered in Amsterdam in 1948 under the theme "Man's Disorder and God's Design." Attention was paid to theological accord and the need for mission. Implications of memberships in the World Council were more clearly worked out at the meeting of the Central Committee in Toronto in 1950. There it was stated that the World Council was not based upon any one particular conception of the church or of the unity of the church. Its role was to be instrumental so that the churches might enter into relation with one another. In 1952 the third World Conference of Faith and Order gathered in Lund.

The second assembly met in Evanston, Illinois, in 1954. The theme, "Jesus Christ—the Hope of the World," set the tone for an assembly at which churches committed themselves to grow together. There was considerable accent on service and somewhat less on mission than at Amsterdam, although evangelization received a great deal of attention.

The third assembly gathered in New Delhi in 1961 under the theme "Christ, the Light of the World." At New Delhi the basis of the Council was changed from "The World Council is a fellowship of churches which accept our Lord Jesus Christ as God and Savior" to "The World Council of Churches is a fellowship of churches which confess the Lord Jesus Christ as God the Savior according to the Scriptures and therefore seek to fulfill together their common calling to the glory of the one God, Father, Son and Holy Spirit." The integration of the International Missionary Council was achieved, and it was decided to admit four Orthodox churches, the churches of Romania, Poland, Bulgaria, and the Patriarchate of Moscow. General Secretary W. A. Visser 't Hooft said on the occasion, "Our ecumenical tasks will not become easier, but we shall surely be greatly enriched." Much attention at this assembly was given to the topic of unity.

Uppsala, Sweden, was the site in 1968 for the fourth assembly. Between the third and the fourth assembly, the fourth World Conference on Faith and Order had met in Montreal in 1963. Nevertheless, Uppsala devoted much of its energy to the rapidly changing world situation. World economic and social development, a strong condemnation of racism, and the financial responsibility of Christians to developing countries were all stressed. This assembly was one third larger than any of its predecessors. Delegates were present from 232 churches in 84 countries. One third of the participants came from the Third World. The largest voting delegation was that of the Orthodox.

The fifth assembly took place in Nairobi, Kenya, in 1975, with the theme "Jesus Christ Frees and Unites." Delegates from 286 churches examined the implications of this theme for the life of the church and the world. Items on the agenda included, "What unity requires." Here a vision of conciliar fellowship was offered to the churches, evangelism was discussed, interfaith dialogue encouraged, the relationship between the unity of humankind and the unity of the church debated. The assembly spoke to the issues of racism, sexism, and human rights. Many recommendations also were made in the light of the technological revolution and its effects on the quality of life.

The most recent assembly of the World Council of Churches, the sixth, was held in Vancouver, Canada, in 1983 on the theme "Jesus Christ—the Life of the World." This theme was subdivided into "Life Confronting and Overcoming Death," "Life in Its Fullness," and "Life in Unity." Delegates from 301 churches, coming from 100 countries, took part in the assembly. Prior to the assembly, the Commission on Faith and Order at its meeting in Lima, Peru, in 1982 completed the convergence document, *Baptism, Eucharist and Ministry.* While the Vancouver assembly did not take any official action on this text, its influence was great and noticeable. The next chapter of the history of the ecumenical movement may well be written on how the churches respond to this statement. Plans call for a fifth World Conference on Faith and Order to be held in 1988 or early in 1989 to review and evaluate the official responses to the convergences claimed by *Baptism, Eucharist and Ministry.*

One of the features that may be noted in the above narrative is the conspicuous absence of Roman Catholic participation. It is true that individual members of the Roman Catholic Church play significant roles in the story described here, but the Roman Catholic Church itself is not involved. This was the situation for much of the time covered in this chapter. In 1928 Pope Pius XI issued the encyclical *Mortalium Animos,* on "Fostering True Religious Union." The document is uncompromising. It rejected Roman Catholic involvement in the ecumenical movement. Unity could come only by the return of non-Catholics to the one true church from which they had fallen away. Nevertheless there were also efforts with Catholicism that sought without repudiating *Mortalium Animos* seriously to understand the ecumenical movement. In their writings, Father Max Pribella and especially Father Y. M. J. Congar represent serious scholarly efforts to articulate a "Catholic" ecumenism. In 1949 the Vatican again defined its attitude to the ecumenical movement in *De Motione Ecumenica.* Although this text recognized the significance of the ecumenical movement, it stated that no Roman Catholics should attend international ecumenical meetings without permission from the Vatican.

All of this changed when Pope John XXIII in 1960 created the Secretariat for Promoting Christian Unity. Now regular contact between the Roman Catholic Church and other churches and the World Council has become possible. Cardinal Bea and his successor as president of the Secretariat, Cardinal Willebrands, have facilitated ecumenical relations. Roman Catholic observers were designated by the Vatican for the New Delhi assembly. Observers from many confessional bodies were permitted to attend the Second Vatican Council. The Degree on Ecumenism which Vatican II adopted in 1964 was a milestone. This decree acknowledges that the cause of ecumenism is indivisible. There is one ecumenical movement. The spiritual gift of the active desire for unity is given for the common good of the whole people of God. After the Second Vatican Council there was no doubt that the entrance of the Roman Catholic Church into the ecumenical movement had irrevocably stimulated and changed ecumenism.

Mention has already been made of the Federal Council of Churches of Christ in America founded in 1905 and its active support of the emerging World Council of Churches. In 1941 a process began that led to the formation of the National Council of the Churches of Christ in the United States of America in December 1950. Fourteen interdenominational organizations, including the Federal Council, the Foreign Missions Conference, Councils for Home Missions, Religious Education, Higher Education, Missionary Education, Stewardship, and the Council of Church Women, merged in a process approved by twenty denominations. Later reorganization changed the Division of Foreign Missions into the Division of Overseas Ministries. In 1960 the National Council moved into its headquarters at the Interchurch Center at 475 Riverside Drive in New York City. In 1981 the National Council amended its preamble to the constitution so as to describe itself not as a "cooperative agency" but as a "community of communions." Presently discussions are continuing about the structure and purpose of the National Council. It may be that in the late 1980s additional changes will be made in the pattern of organization.

In 1944 the Canadian Council of Churches was formed. In 1946 a separate Canadian Overseas Mission Council was established which in 1952 became the department of Overseas Missions of the Canadian Council of Churches. Close relations have developed between the Canadian Council of Churches and the National Council of the Churches of Christ in the U.S.A.

This chapter has traced how Christians have moved from division to greater realizations of the unity they share. As the narrative makes clear, the ecumenical movement has gained momentum in this century. This account of the modern ecumenical movement could leave the impression that ecumenism today is exclusively a matter of church councils. Other portions of this book will make clear that councils are just one important way, but not the only way, that ecumenism is able to bring the churches closer together.

## NOTES

1. A far more complete account of the history described here can be found in Ruth Rouse and Stephen Charles Neill, eds., *A History of the Ecumenical Movement, 1517–1948,* 2d rev. ed. (Philadelphia: Westminster Press, 1967).

2. W. A. Visser 't Hooft, *The Genesis and Formation of the World Council of Churches* (Geneva: World Council of Churches, 1982), 1–8.

# 3

# ECUMENISM—
# AN EXPLANATION

A former archbishop of Canterbury, William Temple, once called the ecumenical movement "the great new fact of our time." And indeed it is. But it is difficult not to question how the understandings of Scripture and the Confessions shared in chapter 1 and the history recounted in chapter 2 have been possible. Have clever theologians and other church leaders devised facile agreements to conceal deep and serious differences? Has one side, under the great economic and social pressures of the modern, post-Christendom day capitulated to the other? This chapter endeavors to answer the question of how the startling ecumenical progress in this century has been possible.

The simplest response is that over the last century and a half tremendous growth in human knowledge and changes in perspective have occurred in virtually every discipline of learning and have in turn created new situations and possibilities that opened the way to concrete ecumenical results. But to appreciate genuinely the ecumenical implications we must look at the wider context.

No one today doubts that the modern world is a place of profound and rapid change. Science and technology have produced vast improvements in transportation and communication, which have brought material growth and educational progress for many. The opportunities of freedom and responsibility given to human beings, who have mobility and material goods once unheard of, have proved to be mixed blessings, for material progress has also produced a nuclear arms race, pollution, and crime. Educational progress has made more people aware of the gaps between the appearance and the reality of such issues as personal freedom, identity, and use of power.

The concept of interdependence has emerged. In the flux of changing and increasing knowledge, old positions were reexamined and often replaced. The natural sciences were deeply influenced by Charles Darwin, who taught that human existence is not simply given but is something worked out through the process of evolution and adaptation. Other natural scientists such as Konrad Lorenz, Loren Eiseley, and Edward O. Wilson have carried Darwin's insights forward. In the social sciences, Sigmund Freud was concerned with the interaction of human behavior and the world within a person. Human existence is not merely a matter of knowing what to do and deciding to do it. There are also unconscious drives, forces, and motives that influence or determine human choices and behavior. Carl Jung and Erich Fromm followed the work of Freud in psychology and developed their own positions. In sociology and economics, attention was given to the social, economic, and political context of the human situation. Karl Marx believed that human problems are the results of alienation from the fruits of one's labor and so from the industrialized world and from the people. Marx insisted that only in and through society can persons live truly human lives. Literature, including the works of Fyodor Dostoevsky, Leo Tolstoy, Arthur Koestler, T. S. Eliot, Georges Bernanos, and countless others, explored a broad and diverse understanding of human existence. Individuals were pictured as people at odds with themselves and others, involved in the struggles to work out their identity in the resolution of conflicts. At the same time, philosophy reflected on the issues encountered in other disciplines. Existentialism, which strives to understand what it means to be human, was represented in the writings of Søren Kirkegaard, Jean Paul Sartre, Martin Buber, and Martin Heidegger. Phenomenology, which concerned the person as knower, was founded by Edmund Husserl and continued by Maurice Merleau-Ponty and Edward Farley. Process thought, stressing the dynamics of all existence, was identified with Alfred North Whitehead. Ludwig Wittgenstein was the principal exponent of positionism, the view that the only possible source of knowledge is sense experience. Following in the tradition of Darwin and Marx, John Dewey taught that human beings are called upon not only to theorize about reality but to change it. According to Dewey, an idea without practical consequences has no real meaning. Pragmatism describes this school of thought. Running through this wide range of approaches to a philosophical understanding of human existence is a common stress on the subjective, the changeable, the particular, and the practical, over against the objective, the unchanging, the universal, and the abstract. Human existence came to be understood, not as a given to be examined, but as a potential in the process of realization.

In the course of the developments in the various disciplines, so superficially related here, modern historical criticism took its present shape. The emphasis of this historical-critical method began in the Renaissance but resulted, especially after the Enlightenment, in a considerable shift in how human beings ask questions, experience reality, understand themselves, and relate to the world. There is a new appreciation of the complexity of human problems and a fresh awareness of the increased amount of knowledge of the world and its past. Today we recognize cultural differentiation, the awareness that different cultures view the world and human life in differing ways and thus express understandings of life in different frameworks. Language is seen in all of its complexity and variety. As a result of all this, there is an acceptance of the fact that there is not just one human way of thinking and speaking, that human beings and their world are not seen as something given, completed, and unchanging. Human experience is seen in developmental terms. The world is not a static essence but is a process of development. In the final analysis, human beings can be understood only in relation to their cultural, historical, and social situations.

Although some Christians initially viewed the development of historical criticism and its implications with alarm, believing that it represented a grave threat to Christianity itself, most, upon reflection and study, have concluded that it has enriched and complicated the theological task of the churches today and that increased knowledge and shifted perspectives have opened up new possibilities for examining traditional questions. The Christian gospel certainly remains the same, but new information and insights provide new resources for confronting modern persons with the gospel and for overcoming some historically divisive problems. The pages that follow offer some general observations about two areas of theology and the changes brought about by the application of historical criticism. The ecumenical implications of these changes in perspective are then examined.

Let us begin with the study of the Bible. In the Middle Ages interpreters of the Bible concluded that the historical context of the Bible was of little, if any, importance. Thus they felt no need or desire to learn about the situations out of which Bible texts arose. For them, allegory was an interpretive method equally appropriate to any biblical text. In contrast, proponents of historical criticism assert that the historical context is of critical importance for an understanding of any biblical passage, that only when a text's meaning for its first readers has been grasped can it be properly understood today. The vast increase in our knowledge about the history, sociology, economics, and languages of the Middle East has helped make such understanding possible.

An examination of the history of theology reveals similar developments. It was once assumed that the Nicene Creed or the Lutheran Confessions were timeless truths that only needed to be repeated. As a result of the historical-critical method, all such documents are now recognized as products of historical development. For proper interpretation, the contexts in which they were written must be taken into account. It is also acknowledged that no one theological vocabulary can be absolutized. Each theological vocabulary, be it at Nicaea or Augsburg, arises in a specific situation for a special task and should be understood in the context of that situation. Much more information about the original context and purpose of such documents is now accessible than was the case even fifty or a hundred years ago. As a result, the original message and intent of many theological documents and their authors can be better understood.

The increase in the amount of information at the disposal of the contemporary theological undertaking and the historical developmental way of thinking offer theological tools that enable a person to interpret the Bible and the history of theology more effectively. A standpoint is provided for a meaningful discussion with modern thought about humankind and its problems. At the same time, earlier theological work continues to have great value. The problems of theology are consistent from age to age. Ignorance of earlier work on these problems is never justified and makes any theologian only poorer. Nevertheless the shift from substantialist and static thinking to dynamic categories and the knowledge explosion makes new resolutions possible as theological problems are viewed in a new light and from a different perspective. This shift of view and spectacular expansion of knowledge explain how ecumenical progress has taken place in this century, as a more in-depth survey of several areas of theology will document.

Perhaps nowhere in theological study is the effect of historical criticism more evident than in biblical study.[1] In general terms, it may be stated that the beginnings of this method can be detected in the Renaissance and the Reformation. Using all the means that the humanists had developed—such as philology, a critical text, and historical study—Luther affirmed that in its literal sense the Bible was clear and open to everyone. Yet Luther also insisted on the necessary role of the Holy Spirit in interpretation. Where a choice must be made between various interpretations, Luther maintained that Scripture should be interpreted from its center: Christ. Thus the Reformation resulted in the Bible exercising a critical function in the church by being the final authority over any office or council. In the next century, science, history, and philosophy became independent subjects. The result was a new way of acquiring knowledge that in turn influenced biblical interpretation. The seventeenth century brought rules of criticism, methodological doubt, restriction of biblical authority by science and history, and an increased role of reason over revelation. All these tendencies came to fuller development with the Enlightenment. Historical criticism developed and found a place in the church. A historical interpretation of the Bible reflecting interest in the origins of biblical documents came into existence. The historical character of revelation and doctrine was acknowledged, and true historical study to understand the past prevailed. The time-conditioned historical character of the Bible was recognized. The significance of the nineteenth century, a time of intellectual and social revolution, for biblical interpretation is difficult to overstress. Historical criticism became a standard approach to understanding the Bible. The unity of the Bible was no longer presumed. Variety in the Bible was stressed. Historical criticism had little appreciation for the category of revelation, but this optimism was challenged by World War I. Individuals such as Karl Barth issued a call for theological interpretation stressing that while historical criticism is a valuable tool, it is only a preliminary step in interpretation of the Bible.

By 1945 historical criticism was firmly in place, but its dangers for faith were obvious. The relationship of faith and historical method was a continuing problem. But as a method, historical criticism was assumed in most circles. While unclarity remained about the exact meaning of historical criticism, or the historical method, most scholars would be in agreement with the definition of Ulrich Wilckins:

> The only scientifically responsible interpretation of the Bible is that investigation of the biblical texts that, with a methodologically consistent use of historical understanding in the present state of its art, seeks via reconstruction to recognize and describe the meaning these texts have had in the context of the tradition history of early Christianity.[2]

Using secular history, textual criticism, philology, literary criticism, form criticism, and redaction criticism, biblical scholars seek to discover the truth and explain what happened within the Bible. In the process, the critical biblical scholars question the text and themselves, and their methods and conclusions. Despite some contrary claims, historical criticism does not disturb true faith. Faith is response to a promise, not acceptance of historical data. Historical criticism, like all human enterprise, stands under sin. It has been misused. Some have claimed too much for it. Nevertheless, historical criticism in the service of the gospel and the mission of the church has brought great ecumenical promise to divided Christians. As the participants of the U.S. Lutheran–Roman Catholic dialogue have declared, "Historical criticism, though by no means the supreme arbiter, must be used as a gift from God in the contemporary discussions among Christians."[3]

Even this concise survey reveals that the impetus for historical criticism and its development were almost exclusively in the hands of Protestants. Roman Catholic involvement in, or use of, the historical-critical method was conspicuously absent until the twentieth century. This is not accidental. Because of the origin of the method and many of the abuses invoked in its name, officially the Roman Catholic Church was hostile to the method for many years. In fact, between the years 1900 and 1940, the Roman Catholic Church took a position against historical criticism. Between 1905 and 1915 the Pontifical Biblical Commission published a series of conservative decisions on the composition and authorship of the Bible. These opinions remained in force until 1943, when a redirection of Catholic biblical studies began. Pope Pius XII released his encyclical *Divino Afflante Spiritu* which noted the misuses of historical criticism, especially by modernism, but also encouraged Catholic scholars to use the historical method and newly discovered texts and materials to study the Bible and to translate it from the original Hebrew and Greek. In 1964 the Pontifical Biblical Commission issued "Instruction on the Historical Truth of the Gospels." It dealt openly with the delicate question of how accurately the Gospels report the words and deeds of Jesus. The Commission made clear that the Gospels are not literal, chronological records of the words and deeds of Jesus but products of a development through years of preaching, selection, and explication. In 1972 Pope Paul VI named as members of the Pontifical Biblical Commission scholars who were committed to historical criticism. Perhaps nowhere more clearly can the commitment of the Roman Catholic Church to modern biblical studies be seen than in the final schema on Revelation (*Dei Verbum*) of Vatican II from the year 1965.[4]

Modern biblical study has not only been characterized by the shift of view represented in historical criticism. It has also been shaped by considerable contributions from new data acquired in the study of ancient languages, history, and archaeology. The deciphering of hieroglyphics and cuneiform, accomplished only in the last century, has yielded information from Egyptian, Babylonian, and Assyrian records. The discovery and decipherment in this century of Ugaritic has produced new understandings of the Hebrew language. The Dead Sea Scrolls and Greek papyri cast new light on the intertestamental and New Testament periods. Other historical discoveries have supplemented the Bible as the only firsthand witness to the great civilizations of the Middle East that preceded Greece and Rome. From Egyptian, Assyrian, and Babylonian documents, Israel's place in the Middle East and the nature of books like Jonah and Daniel are better understood. Newly discovered records of the Roman Empire in Greece and Asia Minor provide previously unavailable historical background to the New Testament. Similarly, modern archaeology, which in Palestine began only in 1890, has elucidated virtually every detail of life in biblical times. All these areas of study have deepened theological perceptions of the wealth and variety of the Bible.

As a consequence of modern biblical studies, characterized by appropriate use of historical criticism and increased knowledge of languages, history, and archaeology, the Bible has become a resource for Christian unity rather than a source of division as it has been so unfortunately often in the past. Critical biblical studies open the door to evaluating the elements of truth in each of several positions and to recognizing that the "either/or" approach of past theological debates often missed the possibility of capturing the truth of both positions. In addition, these studies have made clear that many of the traditional divisions among Christians are products of postbiblical theological development or a precritical reading of the Bible. Two examples may quickly be mentioned. The structure of the church has been one of the traditionally divisive problems for Christians. Is it hierarchical or nonhierarchical? Central to this discussion is the theory that the episcopate is a development of a later period and marks a Hellenistic intrusion on the free charismatic structure of the New Testament church. Historical studies have allowed Catholic and Protestant scholars to widen the theological consensus on the constitution of the New Testament church. Catholic theologians now recognize the growth of church organization through the centuries and a gradual clarification and specification of episcopal and papal powers. They see today anachronisms in an identification of external features of the later church with the New Testament church. Protestant scholars acknowledge the description of simplicity and charismatic freedom in the primitive church as simplistic and not fitting all the available evidence. Such insights clearly have ecumenical import for the dialogue between Roman Catholics and Protestants.

The development of modern historical criticism and the expansion of available knowledge in biblically related fields have created modern biblical studies. Today Roman Catholic, Orthodox, and Protestant scholars in this discipline are acquainted with one another. They know each other's writings, belong to the same learned societies, and contribute to the same scholarly publications. They meet as friends.

# AN EXPLANATION

Differing opinions within their scholarly field are not always deter-mined by denominational labels. The shift of perspective and the knowledge explosion have made modern biblical studies, and other areas of theological study as well, disciplines of great ecumenical accomplishment and promise.

These same two factors of historical criticism and expanded knowledge have created ecumenical possibilities in the field of histor-ical theology. Perhaps nowhere has this been more surprising and more encouraging than in modern studies about Martin Luther, the instigator of one of the major divisions in the history of the church. For centuries two caricatures of Luther prevailed. One pictured him uncritically as a great hero virtually without blemish or flaw. The other saw little good in Luther, viewing him as a heretic with no redeeming qualities, religious or personal. Quite naturally these por-traits were drawn along denominational lines, and there appeared little likelihood that Luther would ever be anything but a stumbling block on the road to unity among Christians. Even in the beginning of this century such Catholic scholars as Heinrich Denifle and Hartmann Grisar refused to take Luther seriously as a religious figure; they viewed him as the heretic who destroyed the unity of the church. But in 1939 when the Roman Catholic scholar Joseph Lortz published his *Die Reformation in Deutschland,* this long-standing view of Luther began to change. Luther studies would never again be the same. By careful scholarship and the use of historical criticism, Lortz broke with past judgments of Luther and held that the Roman Catholic Church could not avoid some share in the responsibility for the tragic events of the sixteenth century. Lortz believed that while Luther was unduly subjectivist, he was nevertheless an unwilling rebel—in fact, an individual whose understanding of the core of Catholicism was frustrated by an institution which at the time was not itself com-pletely representative of Catholicism. Lortz continued to develop his position and in later writings came to even more positive evaluations of the Reformation. But for all his considerable contributions, Lortz still held a view of Luther that was limiting. For Lortz, Luther was one-sided; he made certain doctrines absolute. Thus Luther could be excused in the light of the sixteenth-century Reformation, although to what extent, remained an open question. But for Lortz, although

Luther can be excused, he cannot be a partner for theological conversation. Only in later Roman Catholic scholarship on Luther will he be seen as such.

A number of students carried forward Lortz's pioneering work with significant writings of their own. Ludger Meier, Hubert Jedin, Albert Ebreter, and Erwin Iserloh are representatives of this new Catholic scholarship devoted to Luther. Peter Manns has emerged as one of the most important members of Lortz's school. Manns' biography of Luther, entitled *Martin Luther,* appeared in 1983 during the celebrations of the five hundredth anniversary of Luther's birth and repeated his earlier suggestion that Luther be considered as "a father in the faith," a most remarkable category to be proposed by a Roman Catholic theologian, but one indicative of present Catholic scholarship. Otto Pesch, another Catholic theologian, has argued that Luther should be regarded as a "teacher of the church." Like Manns, Pesch has emerged as one of the most significant Luther scholars with major works on Luther and Thomas Aquinas and the doctrine of justification. All the details of current Luther research cannot be mentioned here,[5] but some tendencies become clear. Systematic study of Luther is now being conducted in an effort to understand his questions and to discover possibilities for consensus between Luther and Catholic theology. In spite of criticism on individual points, Catholic theology is trying to take Luther seriously as a resource for its own theological growth. Luther certainly has not ceased to be a point of disagreement between Christians as a consequence of this process of scholarship, but on many individual points, contradictions between Roman Catholics and Lutherans have lost their sharpness as it becomes clear that the thought structures which condition these points are legitimately Christian, whether they are Catholic or Lutheran. Thus Martin Luther, the theologian, preacher, and reformer, today can be considered as an ecumenical resource, not simply a problem. This is due in large measure to the contributions of Catholic research on Luther, which is in turn indebted to historical criticism and ever-increasing information about the sixteenth century.

Similar developments can be observed in regard to the Augsburg Confession of 1530. As noted in chapter 1, the original intent of this primary Lutheran confession was to preserve the unity of the Western church. Unfortunately this did not happen, and for centuries the Augsburg Confession functioned not as a bridge but as a barrier between different groups of Christians. Although never its original purpose, in Lutheranism the Augsburg Confession had taken on the role of a denominational constitution. Then in the mid-1900s signs of change began to occur. In 1958–59 Roman Catholic theologian Joseph Ratzinger introduced his students to the Augsburg Confession. Some nine years earlier Lutheran scholar Peter Brunner had issued a call for some kind of Catholic recognition of the statements of faith in this confession. By 1976 Catholic theologian Vinzenz Pfnüt had, in several important papers and articles, explored the possibility of recognition of the Augsburg Confession by the Roman Catholic Church. This idea was brought to the attention of the Secretariat for Promoting Christian Unity in Rome and met with initial interest and encouragement. In the same year, Joseph Ratzinger presented a careful and influential lecture in Grau in which he took up the idea of recognizing the Augsburg Confession as Catholic.[6] As a result of these developments a remarkable situation occurred. In the sixteenth century when the Augsburg Confession was proposed as a basis for unity the Roman Catholic Confutation rejected that possibility. Now, four hundred and fifty years later, the Roman Catholics were suggesting consideration of the Augsburg Confession as a Catholic confession. The Lutheran World Federation at its Assembly in Dar-es-Salaam in 1977 indicated great willingness to pursue this idea. By the 450th anniversary year, 1980, and shortly thereafter, an impressive amount of literature had been produced on the "recognition" (*Anerkennung*) of the Augsburg Confession.[7] On 25 June 1980, Pope John Paul II spoke of the Augsburg Confession in a most positive manner. He said, in part, of the sixteenth century and the Augsburg Confession:

> We are all the more grateful that today we see with even greater clearness than at that time, even if there was no success in building a bridge, the storms of that age spared important piers of that bridge. The intense and long-standing dialogue with the Lutheran Church . . . has enabled us to discover how great and solid are the common foundations of our Christian faith. . . . I greet also all Christians . . . on this 450th anniversary of the "Confession of Augsburg," so that from the gospel of creation by God, of redemption in Jesus Christ, and of the call of one people of God, there may develop a new force for a confession of faith full of hope, today

and tomorrow. The will of Christ and the signs of the time are leading us to a common witness in a growing fullness of truth and love.[8]

In reestablishing the original purpose of a confessional document and demonstrating how that document could promote a restoration of unity in diversity, modern scholarship had once again served the ecumenical movement.

It is not only Lutheran figures and documents that have been seen in a new light; many other examples can be furnished. The Council of Trent is one that comes to mind. This Council, considered by the Roman Catholic Church as the nineteenth ecumenical council, embodied the teachings of the Counter-Reformation. It was in session with certain interruptions from 1545 until 1563. While it provided a basis for renewal in the Roman Catholic Church, Trent also seemed, by its rejection of certain Protestant teachings, to foreclose any possible agreements in disputed theological areas. The scholarship of Erwin Iserloh, Hubert Jedin, and August Haler now provides a better understanding of Trent and its later misuse in expressing Catholic theology. These scholars abandoned the idea that the Council of Trent had fixed the norms of Catholic theology, spirituality, and administration forever. Along with others, they sought to put the work and results of the Council into their historical context, and by historicizing them to make clear that what the Council had offered was essentially only temporary solutions to problems which today might require different responses. This work led to a gradual acceptance in the Roman Catholic Church of a historical approach which presented new ways of looking at the Council and paved the way for the teachings of Vatican II. It is now generally recognized that council formulas often stress some aspect of reality that is in discussion at a specific time and place and that needs a special answer. As such, they do not exhaust the whole of Christian truth. The theology of any age, as well as the way in which that theology is expressed, is influenced by the tenor of the times. Also, although council definitions usually condemn or reflect what they regard as error, their positive declarations leave room for the existence of several tendencies and theological positions within orthodoxy. Such an approach has opened up opportunities to overcome some of the divisive teachings by better understanding the exact nature of those teachings and their legitimate limits.

Obviously such a procedure need not be limited to certain councils or teachers. The dialogue between Lutherans and Roman Catholics in the United States has disclosed how Vatican I and its definitions of papal infallibility can be understood today.[9] The use of historical criticism is not a rewriting of history or a means of overcoming serious difficulties irresponsibly, but, as demonstrated in this dialogue, it is a legitimate resource for understanding the original intentions behind many developments in the history of Christianity and for determining their divisiveness today. In his opening speech at Vatican II, Pope John XXIII declared, "The substance of the ancient doctrine of the deposit of faith is one thing and the way it is presented is another." The pope distinguished between a revealed doctrine and its formulation, which led many Roman Catholics to conclude that doctrinal statements of the church are under historical limitation, as are the Scriptures themselves which do not escape the limits of history. Thus while doctrinal formulations of the past capture an aspect of revealed truth, they do not exhaust it. The limited insight of one period of church history can be reexamined in another period of history as Christians use new tools of research or approach truth from a different direction. Roman Catholic theologian Avery Dulles has spoken of the historical relativity of all doctrinal statements.[10]

This view is largely shared in contemporary theology. It is reflected in the statement of the Lutheran Church in America, *Ecumenism: A Lutheran Commitment*. For example:

> In the modern era of ecumenical dialogue Lutherans are learning how to reread their confessions—in their historical context; in light of the Bible as studied today, and through living encounter with representatives of other confessional traditions. They are thus coming to grasp more of the ecumenical potential of the Book of Concord and the intent of all creeds and confessions to give glory to God.[11]

Ecumenical advance can also be explained in part by the impact of historical criticism and the knowledge explosion in other areas of study. Considerable attention has been given recently to the study of language. Many disciplines have been involved: linguistics, anthropology, sociology, medical sciences, and philosophy. Special research has been done on the nature and function of religious language. Attention has been devoted to the way in which symbols, metaphors, and narrative texts function. The distinctiveness of theological language—and even the subdivisions of theological language—has been recognized. The distinctive character of theological language, often best understood as poetry or language of praise, has been acknowledged, as has its cultural conditionedness. Such insights allow theological language to serve its original purpose of doxology or praise of God. Our understanding of theological language no longer restricts it to the presentation of truth claims which equate faith with the acceptance of theological statements.[12] As a result, ecumenical advance is no longer confined to the acceptance of certain set theological formulations, but is freed by an enriched appreciation of the function of language in narrative, poetic, and religious texts.

Finally, no explanation of the ecumenical movement can be regarded as adequate without at least some mention of the liturgical movement. This movement began early in the present century. Its object was to restore the active participation of the people in the official worship of the church. Begun in the Roman Catholic Church, the liturgical movement was soon an important influence in other liturgical churches. Its contributions to ecumenism are many. Several may be mentioned. It encouraged the modern study of the Bible described above. Scholars of many different churches came to know and trust one another as a result of liturgical scholarship, which identified the common elements of worship shared by Christians and encouraged common lectionaries, hymns, and prayer texts. Thus, just as the more technical developments in theology promoted ecumenical progress in official circles and academic settings, the liturgical movement yielded ecumenical activity and growth in congregations and worship communities.

This chapter has supplied an explanation of ecumenism by the description of a theological method that is characterized by the following:

1. The recognition of the ambiguity of all theological statements

because of the inadequacy of human language to comprehend the Transcendent.

2. The acknowledgment of the need to find new language and concepts to express Christian belief.

3. The acceptance of a view of relative emphasis that certain doctrines from the past may no longer be as crucial to the essentials of the Christian message.

4. The approval of legitimate diversity in the interpretation of doctrine so that the same mystery of faith can be differently expressed.

5. The willingness to hear the gospel afresh and clarify or modify denominational traditions in view of that gospel.


NOTES

1. The history of the application of historical criticism to Scripture is available in two accessible volumes: Peter Stuhlmacher, *Historical Criticism and Theological Interpretation of Scripture* (Philadelphia: Fortress Press, 1977); Edgar Krentz, *The Historical-Critical Method* (Philadelphia: Fortress Press, 1975).

2. Ulrich Wilckens, "Über die Bedeutung historischer Kritik in der modernen Bibelexegese," *Was heisst Auslegung der Heiligen Schrift?* (Regensburg: Friedrich Pustet, 1966), 133, cited by Krentz, *The Historical-Critical Method,* 33.

3. Paul C. Empie and T. Austin Murphy, eds., *Papal Primacy and the Universal Church* (Minneapolis: Augsburg Publishing House, 1974), 42.

4. See "The Dogmatic Constitution on Divine Revelation," chap. 3, in *Documents of Vatican II,* ed. Austin P. Flannery (Grand Rapids: Wm. B. Eerdmans Publishing Co., 1975), 756–58.

5. For references to the works mentioned here and a survey of the current state of Luther scholarship, see Peter Manns and Harding Meyer, eds., *Luther's Ecumenical Significance* (Philadelphia: Fortress Press, 1984), and Peter Manns, ed., *Zur Lage der Lutherforschung Heute* (Wiesbaden: Franz Steiner, 1982).

6. Joseph Ratzinger, "Prognosen für die Zukunft des 'Okumenismus,'" *Bausteine* 17, no. 65 (1977), and "Anmerkungen zur Frage einer 'Anerkennung' der Confession Augustana durch die katholische Kirche," *Munchen. Theologische Zatzeitschrift* 29 (1978): 225–37, reprinted in Joseph Ratzinger, *Theologische Prinzipenlehr* (Munich: Erich Wewel, 1982), 230–50.

7. For example, in English see Joseph A. Burgess, ed., *The Role of the Augsburg Confession: Catholic and Lutheran Views* (Philadelphia: Fortress Press, 1980), and George W. Forell and James F. McCue, eds., *Confessing One Faith: A Joint Commentary on the Augsburg Confession by Lutheran and Catholic Theologians* (Minneapolis: Augsburg Publishing House, 1982).

8. Lutheran World Federation News Service Release 27/80 (June 1980), 8.

9. Paul C. Empie, T. Austin Murphy, and Joseph A. Burgess, eds., *Lutherans and Catholics in Dialogue: Teaching Authority and Infallibility in the Church* (Minneapolis: Augsburg Publishing House, 1978).

10. Avery Dulles, *The Survival of Dogma* (Garden City, N.J.: Doubleday & Co., 1971), 173.

11. *Ecumenism: A Lutheran Commitment* (New York: Lutheran Church in America, 1982), Sec. 1.

12. See Peter C. Hodgson and Robert H. King, eds., *Christian Theology* (Philadelphia: Fortress Press, 1982), 23–25, and 56–57; Geoffrey Wainwright, *Doxology: The Praise of God in Worship, Doctrine, and Life* (New York: Oxford University Press, 1980), and the important study by George A. Lindbeck, *The Nature of Doctrine: Religion and Theology in a Postliberal Age* (Philadelphia: Westminster Press, 1984).

# 4

# ECUMENISM
# IN COUNCILS

In chapter 2 we traced the history of the ecumenical movement and the emergence of councils of churches. Now we will focus on two of these councils, the National Council of the Churches of Christ in the United States of America (NCCC) and the World Council of Churches (WCC), and explain their structures and how they function. Although both ecumenical organizations are sometimes the focus of news coverage that is quite critical, most people know surprisingly little about how they actually work.

Let us deal first with the NCCC. It came into existence in December 1950 as the result of a merger process of several ecumenical agencies, and was approved by twenty denominations. Since 1960, the National Council has been headquartered at 475 Riverside Drive in New York City, which is also the U.S. headquarters of the WCC and which houses a number of denominational home offices and religious organizations. Although it has gone through several structural reorganizations, in many ways the NCCC's organizational pattern in 1984 reflects the various agencies that formed it in 1950. This richness of approach has been a valuable resource, but it has also made it difficult to develop a coordinated life within the National Council.

The NCCC is a vital expression of the ecumenical movement in the United States today, but it is not the entire movement. There are still some ecumenically committed churches, such as the American Lutheran Church and the Roman Catholic Church, that do not belong to the NCCC, although they do maintain cooperative relationships with many areas of the National Council's work. The thirty member communions that compose the NCCC nonetheless reflect a wide spectrum of church life in the United States, including Orthodox, Quaker, Reformed, Episcopal, Disciples, Lutheran, Baptist, Presbyterian, Methodist, Moravian, and Swedenborgian Christians. Churches, not individuals, join the National Council, but it is important to remember that the National Council is not a super church. It is, in fact, not a church at all but an organization whose purpose is to provide a place for its member denominations to work together. As the most recent amendment to the preamble of its constitution in 1981 puts it, the National Council is "a community of communions." It is presently trying to define, in a systematic way, what this means for its life and that of the churches which make up its membership.

Sometimes the concern is raised that the National Council will commit its members to programs and policies that are unacceptable to them. But the National Council speaks to and with its member denominations, not for them, and its constitution offers a safeguard against potential abuse of this principle. In Article V, Section 2, it states:

> The Council shall have no authority or administrative control over the churches which constitute its membership. It shall have no authority to prescribe a common creed, form of church government, or form of worship, or to limit the autonomy of the churches cooperating with it.

The National Council is intended to be an instrument for the churches. When statements or policy decisions displease the member churches, two things should be kept in mind. First, the National Council cannot bind its members. The only authority of its pronouncements or actions lies in their inherent worth. Second, the National Council is not a "they" over and against the "we" of the churches. Its boards, committees, and commissions are comprised of individuals selected by and representative of the member churches. The executive staff is elected by representatives of the member churches. Both the member churches and the National Council must strive to make this relationship clear to the denominational membership and the general public, so that the National Council is not misunderstood or misinterpreted.

The NCCC's work is many-faceted. It is a mechanism that enables the member communions to manifest more fully the oneness of the church, to encourage the use of the Bible, to carry on programs of renewal in the life and mission of the churches, to further works of Christian love and service throughout the world, to study and speak on conditions and issues in the world that involve moral, ethical, and spiritual implications of the gospel, and to encourage cooperation among local churches and further the development and support of regional and local ecumenical agencies. In undertaking all of these activities the NCCC establishes and maintains consultative and cooperative relationships with many ecumenical organizations, including the World Council of Churches, but it is neither a structural part nor a subdivision of that world body.

Over the years, as the NCCC has pursued these goals it has provided billions of pounds of food, clothing, and health supplies to the needy, has continued revision of the Revised Standard Version of the Bible, which was translated originally under NCCC auspices, and has promoted dialogue and built relationships among local black churches and between black and white churches. Naturally not every task the NCCC has undertaken has been carried out perfectly, but although it has made mistakes, its cooperative ministry has been and continues to be a valuable gift to many millions.

The policies of the NCCC are determined by a Governing Board composed of 266 persons who are representative of the member churches in proportion to their size relative to the total membership of the National Council. In one sense, the overall governance of the NCCC resides with this Governing Board, which normally meets twice a year. In another sense, governance of the organization is dispersed throughout its program units and committees. Nevertheless its governance always derives from parallel member or eligible-for-membership denominational parts. The Governing Board sets policy and the theological base on social issues and speaks on those issues. It receives or approves the administrative policy, approves budgets after a review by the Executive Committee, and sets the structure of the National Council. The Governing Board has the authority to veto actions undertaken by units of the National Council, but this is rarely, if ever, done. The officers are elected by the Governing Board. Bishop Philip R. Cousin of the African Methodist Episcopal Church is president and Dr. Claire Randall is the general secretary. In November 1984, Bishop Philip R. Cousin and Dr. Arne Brouwer were elected respectively president and general secretary for the period from 1985 to 1988. In 1983 Dr. Randall had indicated her desire to retire at the end of 1984.

Members of the Executive Committee are drawn from the Governing Board and include a constitutionally prescribed number of heads of communions. Upon the recommendation of its four support committees—Personnel; News and Information; Finance and Services; and Research, Evaluation, and Planning—this Executive Committee approves administrative policy, oversees the administration of the National Council, approves the budget, and oversees planning and information policies.

One of the Governing Board's major responsibilities is to speak and act on public policy issues that affect the society and the world in which the churches live and seek to be faithful people of God. Policy positions of the National Council are expressions of the Council and outline its basic policy conviction or position with respect to Christian principles and their application to today's society and world. Their purpose is threefold: (1) to guide the National Council in its program operations, (2) to advise and enlighten the member churches, and (3) to influence public opinion. A proposed policy statement may come to the Governing Board in several ways. Often it comes from one of the National Council's program units or committees. Before a statement becomes policy, two readings and approval by at least a two-thirds vote of the Board members present and voting are required. The process is designed to allow for critical comment and revision. Since 1951 the National Council has issued policy statements on a wide range of topics, including arms control, human rights, the status of women, poverty, Vietnam, the Middle East, and energy. The Governing Board also issues, by a less complex process, resolutions and messages to the churches.

The programmatic life of the NCCC is divided into three functional divisions and five commissions, each of which represents a tie to a historic stream of ecumenical life that became a part of the NCCC in 1950. Divisions are multifaceted and serve a number of functions. The Commissions have more specialized functions. Operating under the policies established by the Governing Board, the various program units set the programs and projects and carry on the detailed work. This work is accomplished through committees, working groups, task forces, and departments of the divisions and commissions. Members of the unit committees of the divisions and commissions are recommended to the Nominating Committee by the member churches and are elected by the Governing Board for a three-year term. Often the program units will include among their members representatives from churches that, though not currently members of the NCCC, are eligible for membership. The Division of Overseas Ministries has on its committee representatives of ten churches that are not members of the NCCC, including the Church of God, the Lutheran Church—Missouri Synod, and the Mennonite Church. Persons with special expertise appropriate to the work of the unit may also be elected as members.

The programmatic units of the National Council as it is structured in 1984 include the following:

The *Division of Overseas Ministries* guides and develops ecumenical mission and service activities and keeps a liaison with each of the regions of the world. This division, which includes Church World Service, accounts for over 80 percent of the financial resources of the NCCC's budget. Its membership comes from the mission and service units of the member churches.

The *Division of Church and Society* has two facets, one related to the domestic mission and the other to concern for socioeconomic justice in the United States. Its members are drawn largely from the American missions and church in society units of the member communions.

The *Division of Education and Ministry* acts as an enabler for the educational ministry programs of the churches and works for quality education in the society. Its members come from the church educational units, and the missionary education and ministry in higher education units of the member communions. It is this division that holds the copyright to the Revised Standard Version of the Bible.

The *Commission on Regional and Local Ecumenism* performs the communication function and serves as a network/liaison between local and regional ecumenical life and the National Council. The Commission is divided into two parts: (1) *Partners in Ecumenism,* which is responsible for the development of ecumenical relations with black churches and (2) *Christian-Jewish Relations.* This Commission's membership is drawn from the member churches and representatives from local and regional ecumenical agencies.

The *Commission on Faith and Order* provides an arena for theological dialogue and provides theological expertise for all the units of the National Council. Its members include persons teaching and involved in theological research and the ecumenical officers of the member communions. Faith and Order has a subgroup responsible for Christian-Muslim relations. The Roman Catholic Church is fully involved in the work of this Commission.

The *Commission on Communication* is a liaison between member churches and the radio and television industry as well as a forum for dealing with the broader communication issues in government and society. Members come from the communications offices of the denominations and from local ecumenical communications groups.

The *Commission on Stewardship* enables member communions to work together in developing common approaches to the stewardship ministry of the churches. Its membership is largely drawn from the stewardship and mission promotion staffs of the churches.

The *Commission on Justice and Liberation* is charged with the responsibility of monitoring the life and work of the NCCC and all of its parts in terms of Third World concerns. Members come mainly from Third World and minority concerns staffs within the member churches.

The General Secretary is the chief executive and as an officer is elected or reelected every three years. The executive staff, which numbers about ninety persons, is elected for an indefinite period with a specific job description. It is the Office of the General Secretary that has overall responsibility for the executive and support staff, and for the administration and work of the National Council. This office also has responsibility for the functioning of the Governing Board and its standing committees. When special programmatic functions emanate from the Governing Board or the Executive Committee, they are either carried out by the Office of the General Secretary or delegated to an appropriate unit. Past and current examples include the Coordinating Council on Hunger concerns and the Committee on U.S./USSR Church Relations. Governing Board panels also do work that may have programmatic implications, for example, studies on the Middle East and on recombinant DNA technology. The Washington Office is a part of the Office of the General Secretary, serving the units of the NCCC, the Governing Board, and member churches for the purpose of advance information and communication. Each division or commission of the NCCC has an associate or assistant general secretary who is accountable both to the General Secretary and to the unit's constituent committees which are made up of persons from the communions.

Of course, in order to perform its assigned task, the National Council needs to acquire funds. Its financial resources come from several sources, including member and related communions, individuals, foundations and corporations as grants, and from the United States Government as service contracts. Some revenue is obtained from the sale of goods and services and from investment earnings.

The financial resources obtained through these various sources are generally restricted to a particular unit and may be designated for a specific purpose. Some funds come as undesignated, in which case they may be restricted to a particular unit or office, but may be used for any purpose by that entity. Most of the resources of the National Council are restricted to a particular unit and designated by the donor for a specific purpose.

Financial support comes by solicitation. Member churches fund at the level of the appropriate NCCC unit. To give one example, the Commission on Regional and Local Ecumenism received financial support from the Division for Mission in North America of the Lutheran Church in America. Individuals are also requested to support the work of the National Council. Church World Service in the Division of Overseas Ministries regularly solicits finances from interested and supportive persons. As part of their membership in the NCCC, member churches are asked to supply support for the Office of the General Secretary and related offices. This support is known as the Fair Share Asking. The amount from each church is determined by a formula approved by the Governing Board, which utilizes the membership figure and the budget of each communion as factors. The amount of financial support given to the NCCC usually amounts to only a few cents a year per member of the member churches. The churches make the decisions about what programs they wish to fund and at what levels and designate funds accordingly. Increasing the level of financial support from the member communions and achieving a more unified budget are certainly among the more serious challenges facing the National Council. In addition to careful monitoring of financial support by most churches, the Office of Finance and Services of the Council keeps a listing of all the Council's resources. Reports showing detailed transactions, summaries, and budget information are produced monthly. The accounting system is audited annually by an independent audit firm. The NCCC operates by fiscally responsible accounting procedures. Budgets are developed from "the bottom up" and not from "the top down." This process enables the Executive Committee and the Governing Board to monitor the decisions reached by the subunits and units. The only monies directly controlled by the core administration, the Executive Committee, or the Governing Board are funds from the Fair Share Askings. These are also allocated to units designated by the Governing Board.

As individuals learn more about the operation and programs of the NCCC, they recognize many of the unfortunate caricatures of the National Council for what they are and discover that the NCCC is a structure through which a diverse, inclusive group of churches struggle to be a flexible and effective instrument for church unity, witness, planning, and action.

But even its most ardent supporters acknowledge the NCCC's shortcomings and the need for improvement. Thus for the last few years a Presidential Panel has been at work to propose a design for the future which will make the National Council a more effective "community of communions." It may well be that in 1990 the description of the NCCC given here will be replaced by a new structural design. If this occurs, one of the major reasons will be a heightened ecumenical commitment on the part of many of the member churches and a desire to see the NCCC become a more responsible and effective resource for their life together.

In much the same way that the National Council seeks to serve American churches, the World Council of Churches (WCC) endeavors to be an instrument of its member churches on the world level. As might be expected, there are some obvious similarities and differences between these two organizations.

The story of the creation of the World Council of Churches has been described in chapter 2, so it will not be repeated in detail here. Suffice it to say that in 1948 in Amsterdam two major strands of the ecumenical movement—Life and Work, and Faith and Order—came together in a new ecumenical organization as 147 churches constituted the World Council of Churches, completing the long process of formation that had been interrupted by World War II. The World Council established its permanent headquarters in Geneva, Switzerland, under the leadership of its first General Secretary, W. A. Visser 't Hooft.

In its early history the World Council was largely a European and North American enterprise, but it has changed over the years. In 1961 the International Missionary Council united with the WCC, followed in 1971 by the World Council of Christian Education. The Western Protestant character of the WCC began to be affected by an increasing number of Orthodox, Pentecostal, and African churches that joined the World Council. Within the last twenty-five years many churches of Asia, Africa, Latin America, the Pacific, and the Caribbean took up membership. Ever-greater roles in the leadership and life of the WCC have been played in recent years by women, laypersons, and youth. The World Council has become an impressive forum of some four hundred million Christians whose churches have entered this fellowship "which confess the Lord Jesus as God and Savior according to the Scriptures and therefore seek to fulfill together their common calling to the glory of one God, Father, Son and Holy Spirit" (WCC, Constitution, Basis). Though not a member, the Roman Catholic

Church shares in several cooperative ventures with the WCC and is officially represented on two of its commissions.

A truly international expression of the ecumenical movement, the WCC is a diverse group of churches, composed of all races, speaking hundreds of languages, and living under extremely different political, social, and economic circumstances. Sometimes it is difficult for North Americans to appreciate or understand the World Council. Often this is because they believe that it must think and act like a North American organization. But it is an international forum with all the strengths and weaknesses of that type of pluralistic group. No one church or group of churches is able to impose its will on the WCC. A helpful analogy might be the United Nations, where Western countries often encounter agendas and priorities other than their own and must engage in genuine dialogue on these other points of view. Seen in this way, the World Council of Churches can be better appreciated and judged on its own merits. It is not an infallible organization, but for 303 member churches, and many others, the WCC is an effective instrument in the search for visible unity of the churches and in common witness and service. Unfortunately, the World Council has frequently been falsely portrayed, often through its own inability to interpret itself accurately. The World Council and its member churches must become better witnesses to its work, so that its true contributions can be praised and its failures redressed.

In its servant role to the churches—the WCC makes no claim to be a church—the World Council seeks to perform five main tasks. They are to (1) call the churches to the goal of visible unity in one faith and eucharistic fellowship; (2) facilitate the common witness of the churches in each place and in all places; (3) support their efforts at common witness and evangelism; (4) express their concern for the service of human need and the promotion of justice and peace; and (5) foster the renewal of the churches in unity, worship, mission, and service. To observe how the WCC accomplishes these functions we must examine its present structure which was put into place in 1971. We will look first at the Assembly and the Central Committee and then at the program units.

The policies of the WCC are determined by delegates of the member churches meeting in an assembly. These assemblies normally are called every seven years. The last such gathering took place in 1983 when the Sixth Assembly of the World Council of Churches met in Vancouver, Canada. Approximately 850 voting delegates gathered with observers, advisers, guests, and staff under the theme "Jesus Christ—the Life of the World." Like any WCC Assembly, this one had three characteristics. First, it was a representative gathering of the member churches and an occasion to reaffirm and celebrate the commitment that the member churches have made to one another. Second, it was an opportunity for the member churches to receive a detailed account of the work of the WCC during the seven years since the last Assembly. Delegates examined the results and formulated recommendations to the WCC and to the churches for further action. Third, as the highest constitutional decision-making and governing body of the WCC, it considered the report of the Central Committee which had directed and supervised the World Council's work since the previous Assembly. From among the delegates it selected members of the new Central Committee as well as members of the Presidium. In Vancouver, Dr. Heinz Held was chosen as moderator of the Central Committee; Dr. Sylvia Talbot and Metropolitan Chrysostomos, vice-moderators. The new presidents of the World Council elected at the assembly include Dr. Marga Buhrig, the Most Rev. W. P. K. Makhulu, Dame R. Nita Barrow, the Very Rev. Lois M. Wilson, Metropolitan Paulos Mar Gregorios, Patriarch Ignatios IV, Bishop Johannes Hempel, and Honorary President Dr. W. A. Visser 't Hooft. The Assembly also received and acted upon policy recommendations in the areas of program guidelines, finance, and public responsibility.

At every assembly of the WCC a Central Committee is elected. The Vancouver Assembly elected a Central Committee of 145 members. This Central Committee meets annually, undertaking more detailed decisions than are possible in an assembly. It is responsible for the operation of the World Council between assemblies. The Central Committee appoints a smaller Executive Committee of about twenty-five persons, including the eight presidents. With a number of commissions and working groups made up of persons with special expertise, this Executive Committee guides the various programs of the WCC.

In 1971 a structure based on three program units—Faith and

Witness, Justice and Service, Education and Renewal—was introduced. These units and the divisions and departments under them will be discussed in detail below. The aim of this restructuring was to make a more effective use of staff and resources, to operate more efficiently and to program priorities more clearly. Even as these changes were made, it was recognized that the work of restructuring the WCC will never be complete. If it is to function as a dynamic and ever-changing body, the World Council will continue to evolve as it does its work for the churches.

## Program Unit 1: Faith and Witness

As its name implies, this unit is concerned with the unity of the church and the content and manner of the witness of its faith in the modern world. It includes Faith and Order, World Mission and Evangelism, Church and Society, Theological Education, and Dialogue with Peoples of Living Faiths and Ideologies.

The *Faith and Order Commission* is concerned with the visible unity of the church. It studies doctrinal and theological issues that still divide the churches and endeavors to give common expression to the Christian faith. In 1982 this commission produced *Baptism, Eucharist and Ministry,* a significant convergence document on these subjects. The churches have been asked to study the document and to make response to several questions raised by Faith and Order. The Faith and Order Commission includes Roman Catholic members.

The *Commission on World Mission and Evangelism* assists the churches in the proclamation of the gospel. Since this means sharing information on evangelism, it persuades the churches around the world to share their resources for mission.

*Church and Society* has devoted attention to the significance of the Christian faith in a world of science and technology. Ethical questions related to such issues as nuclear power, genetics, and environment are studied by this unit.

*Theological Education* replaces the former Theological Education

Fund. It aids the churches to train persons for ministry and mission throughout the world by means of theological schools and alternative programs.

*Dialogue with Peoples of Living Faiths and Ideologies* is a challenging area of work that tries to increase understanding through conversation with Jews, Buddhists, Hindus, Muslims, Marxists, and others.

### Program Unit 2: Justice and Service

This unit stresses the great importance of justice and service within the ecumenical movement. The member churches of the World Council are committed to (1) promoting social, racial, economic, and political justice, (2) helping victims of injustice, oppression, and poverty to meet their basic needs, and (3) supporting these people in the struggle for their fundamental rights. Unit 2 has five subunits.

*Inter-Church Aid, Refugee and World Service* allows the churches to share resources for service. These resources are used to provide medical care, help for scholarships, assistance to churches in minority situations, as well as assistance to victims of human rights violations and those in the midst of natural and other disasters. Refugees are a particular concern of this subunit.

*Churches' Participation in Development* focuses on social justice at all levels of human existence. This commission is committed to solidarity with the poor and seeks economic growth, social justice, and self-reliance through participatory programs involving those it seeks to help. The independently incorporated *Ecumenical Development Fund* makes church investment capital available in the form of low-interest loans to development projects.

*International Affairs* calls the churches' attention to violations of human rights and the dangers of militarism. It encourages the churches to work for the healing of nations through peace and reconciliation.

In 1969 the Central Committee established the *Program to Combat*

*Racism.* This subunit works primarily through specific projects, research, and publications as well as a Special Fund to support organizations of the racially oppressed and other groups with similar aims throughout the world. It holds before the World Council the message that racism is incompatible with the gospel.

The *Christian Medical Commission* stresses community health care, with the accent on people's involvement in their own care as part of their total development. This commission aids in church-related hospitals. Protestant and Roman Catholic churches as well as a number of governmental agencies are involved in its work.

## Program Unit 3: Education and Renewal

Education and Renewal has a threefold task: (1) to stimulate thinking about Christian education, (2) to help make the ecumenical movement effective on the parish level, and (3) to promote the participation of women, youth, and laypersons in church and society.

The subunit *Education* has several main concerns: Bible study, scholarship programs, family life, and childhood.

Another subunit, *Renewal and Congregational Life,* helps local congregations to be centers of worship, life, mission, and service.

A third subunit, *Women,* challenges the WCC and its member churches to foster women's participation in the life of the Christian community. It has programs dealing with the education of women, human rights, and the concerns of women as migrants, refugees, and domestic workers.

The subunit *Youth* encourages young people to explore and live out the Christian faith and to take part fully in the life of the churches and the World Council. It urges the full participation of youth in the work of the WCC.

Coordinating the work of all of these units and providing general leadership is the responsibility of the General Secretariat. Dr. Philip A.

Potter, who became General Secretary in 1972, served in this office until 1984. At the meeting of the Central Committee in July 1984 Dr. Emilio Castro was elected Dr. Potter's successor. Dr. Castro's term as General Secretary began on 1 January 1985. In addition to responsibility for implementing the policies of the World Council as determined by the member churches, the General Secretary provides staff services to the Joint Working Group with the Roman Catholic Church, a group that has been meeting since 1966 to review common concerns and explore possible lines of collaboration. There are also four subunits directly related to the General Secretariat.

The *Communications Department* provides information to the churches and to the wider public about the World Council. It provides translations of documents and simultaneous translation for meetings. It is not uncommon at WCC meetings to have five or six languages used: English, French, German, Spanish, Russian, and Greek.

The *Finance Department* handles the complicated task of controlling WCC finances, working in several world currencies as the Council receives and disburses funds.

The *Ecumenical Institute at Bossey* provides ecumenical leadership training and conducts a Graduate School each year.

The *Library* of the WCC, located at the Ecumenical Center in Geneva, contains an extensive collection of materials dealing with the ecumenical movement.

The last of the subunits related directly to the General Secretariat is the *U.S. Conference of the World Council of Churches.* Located at 475 Riverside Drive in New York City, it maintains relationships with the U.S. member churches and supplies information and research materials.

The General Secretary heads a staff of approximately 300 persons plus a support staff. This staff represents over 40 different countries and still many more churches and traditions. Executive staff is normally elected by the Central Committee. When an executive position is vacant, member churches and Central Committee members are notified and requested to submit names of candidates. Length of service with the WCC varies. The current practice is for executive staff persons to serve for no longer than nine years.

Even such a brief description of the structure of the World Council of Churches as has been given here reflects its many activities. The organization's budget mirrors this same diversity of activities. Every year over $50 million flows through its books, some $40 million of which is earmarked for other destinations—to help victims of various disasters and to support projects ranging from leadership scholarships to evangelism and rural development. The balance of the funds pays for the WCC's own operations and programs. The major contributors to the World Council are the member churches and their mission and aid agencies, although some funds for specific projects come from secular and governmental organizations and foundations. There is no fixed membership fee. The member churches contribute what they can. This varies greatly according to the ability and context of the churches. Some churches, forbidden by government regulations to send money out of their countries, search for other ways to support the World Council. In recent years the toll of inflation, internal budgetary problems of the member churches, and adverse currency exchanges have all created financial problems for the WCC. Nevertheless, many churches made significant increases in contributions during this difficult time. The annual expenditure to the WCC is only a small percentage of the yearly budget for most of the larger churches. Both the member churches and the WCC carefully monitor the financial situation of the World Council. The WCC, for its part, has adopted certain economy measures—for example, reducing staff and limiting travel. Churches tend to participate selectively in the work of the WCC. They fund the General Administration and those activities of special interest to them. A church's membership in the WCC does not mean that it supports or finances every activity of the organization. But membership does rightly acknowledge the unique ecumenical role the WCC plays on the world scene. In spite of the confusion about the WCC and misgivings about some of its decisions, it remains a critical instrument for over three hundred churches around the world as they struggle to live out their commitment to the ecumenical movement. If the member churches wish a better instrumentality to express their ecumenical commitment internationally, then the challenge is before them to make *their* World Council more what they desire it to be.

Conciliar ecumenism is not irresponsible and misguided, as some have suggested. As this concise narrative has shown concerning two ecumenical agencies of the churches, it is an arena of considerable hope for the ecumenical movement. Yet it is not the only arena of such hope, and this brings us to the next chapter.

# 5

# ECUMENISM
# IN DIALOGUE

In the preceding chapter we indicated how two Councils function as ecumenical organizations and allow their member churches to learn to know one another, address issues in the world, and strive to express their unity. Now we wish to describe another form of ecumenical relation that assists churches to put away their past divisiveness and to discover their legitimate diversities and unity. We will be talking about what has come to be known as ecumenical dialogues or bilateral conversations. Both terms are used in this chapter to designate theological conversations undertaken by officially appointed representatives of two churches, two traditions, or two confessional families, with purposes ranging from promoting mutual understanding to achieving full fellowship.[1]

According to this definition, we can expect that these dialogues will have certain presuppositions and features. For example, the dialogue partners are conscious of their own identity or confessional character; the dialogues are official in that they are officially authorized by churches, with officially appointed participants; and dialogues tend to address doctrinal matters, seeking to overcome theological and ecclesiological divergences from the past and to develop agreements. Dialogues share the conviction that theological differences between churches are rooted in their historical heritage and are still operative today. Proponents of bilateral conversations believe that the official nature of these dialogues assists the churches in taking their work seriously.

Dialogues have taken place in the ecumenical movement since before 1960, but it is actually within the last twenty-five years that they have assumed special importance. Significant conversations occurred earlier between Anglicans and Old Catholics, Anglicans and Orthodox, and Old Catholic and Orthodox. These noteworthy efforts, however, pale in comparison to the proliferation of dialogues since the early 1960s. In the past twenty-five years, in fact, dialogues have produced so many new and pioneering agreements that it is an open question whether the level of intensity and productivity can be maintained. Yet this is not to say that the bilateral process has ended. It clearly has not.

The remarkable developments of these dialogues have succeeded in bridging age-old divisions within a short span of time. They pose the intriguing question of why all of this is happening at this particular time. No doubt, those committed to the faith community of Christianity see the workings of God's Spirit. They believe that in the mystery of time God in this age is calling his people to a unity. On the level of observable affairs, several factors may be indicated. Since these factors have been described in earlier chapters, references here will be brief.

First, the ecumenical efforts prior to 1960 created an atmosphere for constructive dialogue between the churches. The conferences of Faith and Order and Life and Work, and the existence of the World Council of Churches, all allowed the churches to overcome past animosities and recognize their common witness on many issues. Probably the discussions of the Commission on Faith and Order have special importance here.

Second, the Second Vatican Council in the 1960s opened a new chapter of ecumenism. It is no accident that dialogues increased significantly in number after Vatican II. Having made the decision to participate in the ecumenical movement, the Roman Catholic Church sought to develop contacts with several church traditions. With its size and resources this resolve had immediate effects on bilateral conversations.

Lastly, the insights in the historical conditioning on the perception and articulation of Christian truth were becoming more widely accepted within mainstream churches by 1960. This freed churches and their dialogue representatives to look in a new way at theological and doctrinal arguments that a generation earlier were considered unshakable. Such arguments could now be regarded with integrity as negotiable or quietly set aside as not useful in the present climate of mutual trust and acceptance between the churches.

Few persons today will deny the valuable and impressive accomplishments of these conversations. Such success should not blind us to some limits of this approach. Some of the very factors that are the strong points for dialogues among some are weaknesses for dialoguing with others. For example, dialogues are easier to initiate and to conduct for churches that are well organized at world, regional, and national levels. Churches without such organizations have difficulty in participating in dialogues and are often left out of bilateral activities. In some instances this has happened simply because it has been impossible to identify an appropriate agency within a tradition that could sponsor such a conversation. Dialogues are most suitable for those churches which possess a strong tradition of, and high regard for, dogmatic theology, doctrinal decisions, formularies, and a well-structured liturgical tradition; thus churches less theological and more experiential in character and message have generally been omitted from dialogues. It should be possible to develop different types of bilateral conversations to include such churches. As Pentecostal and other similar traditions acquire more interest in formal theology, they may find dialogues more congenial. Nevertheless dialogues will probably never be the ideal method of ecumenical advance with some churches, and other ways will have to be found.

Most of the dialogues conducted on the world and national levels have involved Anglican, Lutheran, Orthodox, Reformed, and Roman Catholic communions and have covered such topics as the relation of gospel, Scripture, and tradition; the Lord's Supper; ministry; and mutual recognition of ministries or churches—all items that have tended to be historically divisive between these communions. The agencies or the churches sponsoring a dialogue appoint a number of representatives. Those appointed have generally been professionally educated theologians. Such persons are expected to use their gifts as theologians. But they must maintain an awareness of the official nature of their appointment by the churches. Though they cannot bind their churches, they do have an obligation to reflect their churches' official teachings. Normally a dialogue will meet for several years. It may or may not have a specific mandate from its sponsors.

Topics are usually identified as part of the mandate at a first meeting. Papers are written by representatives, shared and discussed at the regular meetings of the dialogue—usually once or twice a year. Many dialogues have been able to produce convergence statements on the topics discussed, sometimes statements of agreement. At the conclusion of the particular dialogue these materials go to the sponsoring organizations and churches. These dialogue reports do not merely elaborate on consensus, they press toward the realization of some form of ecclesial fellowship between the churches, for dialogues are not content with theological consensus for its own sake but as a mechanism for achieving church unity. For example, they make suggestions to the churches about recognition of ministries or eucharistic sharing. Many of the dialogues, while conducting their work in confidence, publish their papers and statements at the completion of their work, so that their findings can be widely discussed within the church and can serve as a resource to other dialogues.

Here we see a critical characteristic of dialogues: they continually point beyond themselves to a phase where the goal is no longer reaching convergence or consensus but the translation of these theological agreements into practice in living fellowship of churches. These phases overlap, but it appears that the challenge in the 1980s will shift the focus of efforts from the quest for convergence and consensus to more concrete attempts to convert the agreements into fellowship. The question, then, is how participating communions take hold of and evaluate the results of the dialogues and, where appropriate, give them the kind of authoritative character in the churches that will bring about ecclesial fellowship. This must be done in such a way that all arenas of the church are involved: local congregations and their clergy, as well as church leaders, and theologians. It is a question we will discuss more fully in the last chapter of this book.

Ecumenical dialogues have become an area of specialized study in their own right. The amount of material produced by the bilaterals is voluminous. Even the secondary resources can be overwhelming. Fortunately two convenient resources are available for study. The first, *Confessions in Dialogue* by Nils Ehrenström and Günther Gassmann, is available in a third, revised and enlarged edition. This book surveys regional, national, and world-level dialogues, and includes useful chapters on dialogue methods, contributions, and future work. It is an excellent resource, with one limitation. It is now out of date, for much has occurred since the publication of the third edition in 1975.[2] Another book is *Growth in Agreement: Reports and Agreed Statements of Ecumenical Conversations on the World Level,* edited by Harding Meyer and Lukas Vischer.[3] This is actually a collection of dialogue texts with the advantage that it includes material up to 1982. It has the unfortunate restriction of including materials from only world-level dialogues, so that many important regional and national texts do not appear. Nevertheless, together these two books offer a significant overview of bilateral activity.

The remainder of this chapter will offer descriptions of some of the major bilateral conversations that have taken place or are presently in progress. The choice is intended to be representative of dialogue activities, but in a certain sense it is arbitrary. Other equally valuable dialogues could have been selected to achieve our purposes. The particular inclusions or omissions are not intended to signify any relative importance or worth.

## ANGLICAN–ROMAN CATHOLIC DIALOGUE

Anglicans and Roman Catholics have been in dialogue in the United States and on the world level for many years. In the United States the preliminary meeting was held in 1965, and since that time this national dialogue between the Episcopal Church, U.S.A., and the Roman Catholic Church has addressed a number of topics affecting church relations. Considerable agreement has been noted on baptism, the church as a eucharistic fellowship, the theology of the celebrant, and the nature of eucharistic sacrifice. In 1969 the dialogue declared its goal to be full communion and organic unity, and it suggested steps toward this goal. The dialogue commission in 1972 adopted "Doctrinal Agreement and Christian Unity," a set of principles to serve as a guide in appraising doctrinal diversity and change. This may be its most significant contribution. In 1976 an agreed statement on the purpose of the church appeared. As this dialogue continues to meet and work, it has not limited itself to doctrinal questions but includes topics such as worship, church life, and mixed marriages. It has also encouraged local and spiritual ecumenism, calling for local study and response to the national and international agreed statements. As a result of this bilateral a number of joint pastoral letters have been issued by Episcopal and Roman Catholic bishops. Many Episcopal and Roman Catholic dioceses have their own dialogue committees, and a number of covenants between parishes have been put in place. The approach of these dialogues has tended to be simple and pastoral. It is less academically theological than some others, and its results have been published without extensive documentation, position papers, and process descriptions. It has discovered wide areas of convergence and indeed substantial agreement between Episcopalians and Roman Catholics in the United States and has had immediate practical and pastoral ramifications for local ecumenism in both churches. This bilateral is one example of remarkable progress in a short time.[4]

In 1984 a new phase of the Episcopal–Roman Catholic dialogue in the United States began. Changes in membership were made in the Episcopal and Roman Catholic representation. The commission decided to begin a study of the topic of mutual recognition of ministries. Decisions were also made about topics for its future agenda. The subject of formation of conscience in relation to moral issues is to be addressed after mutual recognition.

The beginnings of the international Anglican–Roman Catholic dialogue can be traced back to the March 1966 visit of the Archbishop of Canterbury to Pope Paul VI. This meeting led to the appointment of a joint preparatory commission which met from 1967 until January 1968. The resulting report contained an outline of basic agreements and a number of recommendations, including a list of topics for theological discussion. Its final recommendation was for the establishment of a permanent joint commission. This new commission, later renamed Anglican–Roman Catholic International Commission (ARCIC), held its first meeting in 1970. It was composed of nine Anglican and nine Roman Catholic members, representing both worldwide communions. In 1971 the commission issued the Windsor Statement, a document on eucharistic doctrine which claimed consensus on the affirmation of the real presence without the use of substantialist categories and on an insistence on the "once and for all" of Christ's sacrifice. From 1972 until 1973 ARCIC concerned itself with the topic of ministry. The Canterbury Statement of 1973 took up ministry and ordination. The commission did not continue the old debate of validity of orders but explored common grounds about the nature of the church's ministry. In this process the commission stated that while there might be differences of emphasis in both traditions, they believed that in what they said about ministry, both the Anglican and the Roman Catholic churches would recognize their own faith. One of the thorniest ecumenical subjects became the topic of the next phase of the dialogue's work: the shape of authority in the church, including consideration of the Petrine office. In 1976 the Venice Statement on authority in the church was released. Acknowledging the importance and difficulty of the subject, they nonetheless claimed a consensus, at the same time recognizing that this consensus did not resolve all the problems in this sensitive area. The Commission did insist that acceptance of their work on authority in the church by both communions would have important consequences for future relations.

As early as 1971 and the Windsor Statement, the commission invited comments and criticisms of its work from the churches sponsoring it. In 1979, in the light of these replies, the commission published "Elucidations" on its statements on eucharistic doctrine, and ministry and ordination. The purpose of the "Elucidations" was to expand and clarify these statements in response to these reflections and criticisms from the churches. The commission saw this task as an important part of its work, and there is little doubt that these efforts did refine the reports of the commission and make them more understandable in the churches. In 1981 in a similar manner the commission published an "Elucidation" on its document on authority in the church, the Venice Statement.

The Windsor Statement of 1981, in which the commission deals with authority for the second time, is also the dialogue's last report. This report, the result of five years of further study, addresses four difficulties: (1) the interpretation of Petrine texts in Scripture, (2) the meaning of language of "divine right," (3) papal infallibility, and (4) the nature of the jurisdiction ascribed to the bishop of Rome as universal primate. In addition, the report traced the commission's history, reviewed the documents it produced, and described its work by means of the motif of *koinonia* (communion). The Windsor Statement of 1981 maintains that unity is of the essence of the church and that since the church is visible, its unity also must be visible. It acknowledges that full visible communion between these two churches cannot be achieved without mutual recognition of sacraments and ministry, and common acceptance of a universal primacy at one with the episcopal college in the service of the *koinonia.*

In 1982, after some delay, *The Final Report: Anglican–Roman Catholic International Commission* was published and released to the churches.[5] It contains all the agreed statements, the "Elucidations," and a series of appendices with pertinent background material on the dialogue. This report is now before the worldwide Anglican communion and the Roman Catholic Church for official study and response. In the meantime a new Anglican–Roman Catholic Commission has been appointed. It held its first meeting in Venice in 1983, and, as its first topic, is taking up justification by faith.

## ANGLICAN-LUTHERAN DIALOGUE

The beginnings of Anglican-Lutheran dialogue on the world level can be traced back to 1963 when the Lutheran World Federation passed a resolution calling for a study committee for the preparation of a worldwide Anglican-Lutheran conversation. Contacts with the archbishop of Canterbury resulted in the appointment of an ad hoc committee in 1967. In the same year, this committee prepared a memorandum calling for (1) a worldwide Anglican-Lutheran dialogue, (2) other contacts and practical cooperation, and (3) regular reports to the appropriate authorities.

In 1968 this memorandum was accepted by the Lambeth Conference of the Anglican communion and the Executive Committee of the Lutheran World Federation. The Lambeth Conference suggested that the dialogue should begin with the general mission of the church in the world and then move on to questions of doctrine and order. It also asked that the conversations meet four times during a two-year period. The following year the archbishop of Canterbury and the officers of the Lutheran World Federation appointed their respective delegations. There were nine Lutheran and ten Anglican participants. Both groups included representatives from different areas of the world and with a variety of approaches to theological thinking and church life within the two confessions. A permanent observer from the World Council of Churches was appointed. The four meetings took place at Oxford, England, in 1970; Legumkloster, Denmark, in 1971; Lantana, Florida, in 1972; and Munich, Germany, in 1972. From the beginning the group examined conditions for mutual recognition and fellowship between the two churches. The dialogue investigated sources of authority, the church, the Word and Sacraments, apostolic ministry, and worship. The final report, the Pullach Report of 1972, spoke to these topics and included personal comments by the two cochairmen.[6] The Pullach Report reflects substantial agreement on these subjects, with certain qualifications about the historic episcopate. The existing differences are thought to be the result of differing historical developments and should not be held to be divisive. Although the historic episcopate remains a controversial issue, the gap between the differing positions was greatly narrowed by the acknowledgment that apostolic mission and episcopacy are more basic and inclusive realities than apostolic succession in the particular form of the historic episcopate. Both communions exercise the essential function of oversight in varying forms. This, according to the report, should not prevent mutual recognition. Mutual recognition of the Anglican and Lutheran churches as a true communion of Christ's body possessing a truly apostolic ministry is urged, including intercommunion. After the completion of the dialogue's work, an official Joint Working Group was commissioned by the Anglican Consultative Council and the Executive Committee of the Lutheran World Federation to evaluate the responses of the churches to the dialogue report.

At approximately the same time as the events described above were occurring on the international level, a dialogue between Episcopalians and Lutherans was taking place in the United States. The original invitation was extended by the General Convention of the Episcopal Church, U.S.A., in 1967 and was accepted by the American Lutheran Church, the Lutheran Church in America, and the Lutheran Church—Missouri Synod. The dialogue, sponsored by the then Joint Commission on Ecumenical Relations of the Episcopal Church, U.S.A., and the Division of Theological Studies of the Lutheran Council in the U.S.A., began under its mandate to explore the possibilities and problems for a more extended dialogue to deal with fellowship, unity, or union goals. It was composed of nine representatives from each side. Soon the group, discovering wide areas of unity, went beyond its mandate to explore questions related to altar and pulpit fellowship. It noted agreements on Holy Scripture, the doctrine of the Apostles' Creed and the Nicene Creed, justification by faith, baptism, and the Eucharist, although with differing emphases. As with the international dialogue, the greatest problems centered around the meaning of apostolicity, but even here agreement was deemed sufficient to recommend limited intercommunion. In making this recommendation, the Lutheran participants accepted a position contrary to the orthodox Lutheran view that full doctrinal consensus is required for eucharistic sharing. The dialogue met six times between 1969 and 1972 in Detroit, Milwaukee, St. Paul, and three times in New York. Its final report was prepared in 1972 and published in 1973.[7]

Although the first series of U.S. Lutheran-Episcopal Dialogue (LED) proposed intercommunion, the sponsoring churches took no action on this suggestion. Rather, a second series of dialogues, LED II, was authorized under the sponsorship of the Division for Theological Studies of the Lutheran Council in the U.S.A. and the Standing Commission on Ecumenical Relations of the Episcopal Church, U.S.A. This was prompted by the desire on both sides for more historical and theological support for the conclusions. In addition to the participants in the first series, the Association of Evangelical Lutheran Churches named a representative for the new series. The dialogue met eight times between 1976 and 1980 in various locations in the Midwest and South. In 1981 it released its final report. This document described the history and methodology of the dialogue, contained joint statements on justification, the gospel, eucharistic presence, and the authority of Scripture, and concluded with a series of recommendations and statements to both constituencies.[8] The recommendations asked the churches mutually to recognize one another as true churches, to work out a policy of interim eucharistic hospitality, to encourage the kind of joint worship recommended in the report of the international conversations, to publish and circulate the dialogue reports, to encourage congregational covenants, and to authorize a third series of dialogues on ministry. The participants from the

Lutheran Church—Missouri Synod had their own recommendations which were more modest.

In the light of these recommendations the American Lutheran Church, the Association of Evangelical Lutheran Churches, and the Lutheran Church in America together with the Episcopal Church, U.S.A., began a process of study to see if similar recommendations could be presented to their national conventions. The Lutheran Church—Missouri Synod did not officially take part in this study, but did send an observer-consultant. By January 1982 the four churches officially involved in the study had arrived at a common text of recommendations for their conventions. These recommendations, which became known as the Lutheran-Episcopal Agreement, were approved by large majorities in general conventions of the Episcopal Church, U.S.A., the American Lutheran Church, the Association of Evangelical Lutheran Churches, and the Lutheran Church in America in September 1982. It should be noted that the text of the agreement is not identical with the recommendations of LED I, LED II, or the international dialogue. It is a refinement of the dialogue work and clearly based on them. The Agreement has five parts: (1) a word of appreciation for the dialogues and a commitment to the goal of full communion, (2) a mutual recognition of the churches as churches in which the gospel is preached and taught, (3) an encouragement of the development of common Christian life, (4) the establishment of a relationship of Interim Sharing of the Eucharist, and (5) the authorization of a third series of dialogue.[9] Since the approval of the agreement, response in the churches has been extremely positive. Lutherans and Episcopalians have worshiped and communed together, studied and engaged in joint work. They are not involved in merger with each other. Although all differences have not been solved between them, Episcopalians and Lutherans in the United States believe that they have taken a small step to greater unity. They are eager to share this model with others. Even closer ties between the two traditions will depend on local response to agreement and on the work of the third series of dialogue (LED III) which began in 1983.

In addition to the three series of U.S. dialogues discussed above, other regional dialogues have occurred between Anglicans and Lutherans. One example is the Anglican-Lutheran European Regional

Commission which met three times between 1980 and 1982. Sponsored by the Anglican Consultative Council and the Lutheran World Federation, its final report was prepared in Helsinki in 1982 and published the following year.[10] This report provides an introduction to the dialogue, a historical description of relations between the two communions, an account of the present situation of the two churches in Europe, and recommendations. The recommendations, built on the international and American dialogues, called for mutual recognition as true churches, interim steps toward full communion, occasional mutual participation in presbyterial and episcopal ordinations, pastoral and theological exchanges, and joint local mission and social witness. In some specifics this dialogue moved beyond its American counterparts, but in its general direction and goal it reflected great similarities.

As a consequence of the remarkable convergence that has been developing between the Anglican and Lutheran communions, the Anglican Consultative Council invited the Lutheran World Federation in 1981 to reconvene a joint working group. This initiative was welcomed by the Executive Committee of the Lutheran World Federation in 1982. At the end of 1983 the Joint Working Group met in England. In its report, past and present Anglican-Lutheran relations are viewed. The goal of Anglican-Lutheran dialogue is described as full communion and steps are suggested in moving toward this goal. Specific recommendations are put forth which include endorsement of interim eucharistic sharing as authorized in the United States. The report of the Anglican-Lutheran Joint Working Group dramatically illustrates the progress that has been made in these relationships since 1963.[11]

## LUTHERAN–ROMAN CATHOLIC DIALOGUE

The Lutheran–Roman Catholic dialogue in the United States is the longest continually functioning dialogue commission in America. Its origins go back to informal conversations in 1963 between Roman Catholic Bishop John J. Wright and Dr. Paul C. Empie, the executive director of the National Lutheran Council. In 1965, after two years of discussions, the National Lutheran Council, acting in its capacity as the U.S.A. National Committee of the Lutheran World Federation, and the Roman Catholic Bishops' Commission for Ecumenical Affairs approved a formal dialogue. A planning group met in March 1965. The dialogue itself began in July of that year and has continued to the present. Over the years approximately twelve to fourteen persons have been named by each side as dialogue participants. The Lutheran Church—Missouri Synod, although not a member of the Lutheran World Federation, was invited to send two representatives. It accepted this invitation, and its representatives have taken an active role in the work. After the formation of the Association of Evangelical Lutheran Churches and its acceptance in the Lutheran World Federation in 1977, this church body had one representative on the commission. The individual participants in the dialogue prepare papers on selected topics relating to the theme of the conversation. Occasionally each group will caucus separately to formulate questions for the other group. This helps to establish a basis for directing discussion and finally drafting a joint statement. The usual pattern is for the dialogue to meet for several days twice a year.

Although it is unclear whether the goal of the dialogue was ever officially defined, in practice it has served to explore the theological relationships between the two churches in an effort to discover to what extent the differences that have divided these communions in the past still constitute obstacles to mutual understanding. In the opinion of many, this dialogue has done just that and with considerable success.

At the outset of these conversations the decision was made to begin with topics on which there might be broad areas of agreement and move from there to issues that have been more controversial or divisive. Therefore the dialogue started its work with the role of the Nicene Creed as dogma in the church. It found substantial agreement in confessing the Nicene Creed and made some tentative exploration into the problem of the nature and role of dogma. Representatives in the dialogue quickly agreed that the development of doctrine was a crucial subject for their work. This method of work reveals the traditional Lutheran and Roman Catholic view that the only legitimate grounds for division in the church are doctrinal, and that therefore such differences carry greater weight than differences in practice or cultural conditioning. Upon the completion of their work on the

Nicene Creed the dialogue made the important decision to publish regularly their reports and papers so that they could be studied in the churches. *The Status of the Nicene Creed as Dogma of the Church* appeared in 1965.

The second topic was "one baptism for the remission of sins." Roman Catholic and Lutheran presentations on New Testament material, indicating a common view of baptism as a rite of initiation in the community of faith, demonstrated a consensus which has continued in the historical and doctrinal discussion. Nevertheless, the dialogue noted the question of different theological vocabularies between Lutherans and Roman Catholics and saw once again that the question of the development of doctrine, especially as it relates to the issue of the teaching office of the church, is a critical topic. In 1966 the dialogue published *One Baptism for the Remission of Sins.*

The dialogue commission then turned its attention to two subjects that have been especially divisive in the past: "the Eucharist as sacrifice" and "the mode of Christ's presence in the sacrament." Intensive research and discussion yielded immense progress on "sacrifice" and "presence" in the Eucharist. The dialogue built on the earlier work of the Fourth World Conference on Faith and Order (Montreal, 1963) and much current New Testament and patristic scholarship. It concluded that in spite of the remaining differences in the ways that Roman Catholics and Lutherans speak about and think of eucharistic sacrifice and the Lord's presence in his supper, they should no longer regard themselves as divided in the one, holy, catholic and apostolic faith on these points. Also pointed out was the significant convergence in the practice of eucharistic worship between Roman Catholics and Lutherans. At this time the dialogue did not devote any major attention to the relation between the Eucharist and the teaching office of the church. Both eucharistic ministry and intercommunion were omitted from the discussion, though a commitment was given to take up Eucharist and ministry in the future. *The Eucharist as Sacrifice* was released in 1967.[12]

A reexamination of the possibilities of intercommunion made it clear that no progress would be possible in this area without consideration of what constitutes a valid ministry in eucharistic celebration. Thus the dialogue addressed itself to "Eucharist and ministry." It sought to clear away misunderstandings, to clarify the theological concerns of each tradition, and to see what common affirmations could be made about the reality of the ministry. A distinction was made between ministry and Ministry. The task of the whole church to proclaim the gospel to all is "ministry." On the other hand, "Ministry" is a particular form of service, a specific order, function, or gift (charism) within and for the sake of Christ's church in its mission to the whole world. The Ministry has the responsibility of proclaiming the gospel to the world and building up in Christ those who already believe. The Spirit endows the Ministry with a variety of gifts. Three features of Ministry were discussed: its apostolic nature, entry to it by ordination, and the question of its character. Agreement was found to be possible in all three areas. The dialogue developed a series of recommendations in which Roman Catholics asked their church and Lutherans requested their churches to recognize the validity of the ministry and the eucharistic administration of the other communion. After three years of intensive effort, the Lutheran–Roman Catholic dialogue published *Eucharist and Ministry* in 1970.[13]

Encouraged by the significant results of its studies on Eucharist and ministry, the dialogue pursued the subject of papal primacy. It organized its work around the notion of a Petrine function defined as "a particular form of ministry exercised by a person, office holder or local church with reference to the Church as a whole." This Petrine function was implied in the New Testament, but in its various forms it was subjected to continuous evolution and renewal. The dialogue participants agreed on the following: (1) Christ wills a manifest unity for his church in the world; (2) promotion of this unity is incumbent on all believers; (3) the greater the responsibility of a ministerial office, the greater its responsibility to seek the unity of all Christians; (4) a special responsibility for this may be entrusted to one individual; and (5) ministry under the gospel and such a responsibility for the universal church cannot be ruled out on the basis of the biblical evidence. The renewal of papal structures was viewed as centered around three principles: legitimate diversity, collegiality, and subsidiarity (what can properly be decided and done in some other units of ecclesial life ought not be referred to church leaders who have wider responsibilities). In the final report, the Lutheran churches were asked to consider the possibility and desirability of the papal ministry, renewed under the gospel and committed to Christian freedom in a larger communion which would include the Lutheran churches. The Roman Catholic Church was asked to consider the possibility of a reconciliation that would recognize the self-government of Lutheran churches within a communion and the acknowledgment of Lutheran churches in the dialogue as sister churches that are already entitled to some measure of ecclesiastical communion. *Papal Primacy and the Universal Church* was published in 1974.[14]

From 1973 until 1978 the dialogue grappled with an even more intractable problem in Lutheran–Roman Catholic relations: papal infallibility. The broad-based approach investigated indefectibility of the teaching office, counterparts to infallibility, the authority of councils and creeds, and the psychosocial factors that contributed to the evolution of this doctrine. The common statement refers to the reassessment of popular assumptions and theological interpretations about infallibility since the Second Vatican Council. It points out the great problems of this doctrine for Lutherans. While Lutherans do share with Catholics the conviction that the church of Christ is indefectible, they consider the maintenance of this indefectibility to be the sovereign work of God. To Lutherans the dogma of infallibility as historically formulated appears to be an attempt to usurp the Lordship which God conferred on Christ alone. The common statement proceeds to explain carefully that Lutherans need not exclude the possibility that papal primacy and other teaching authority might be acceptable developments, at least in certain respects. It declares that the theoretical possibility of seeing papal teaching authority in a more favorable light is now being actualized. Roman Catholics are rethinking their position. Thus Lutherans may well have to ask themselves whether the Roman Catholic doctrine of papal infallibility, even if not something that they would be able to affirm for themselves, need continue to be regarded by them as anti-Christian and therefore as a barrier to the unity of the churches. Catholics may well have to ask themselves whether their view of the papal teaching office and its infallibility can be so understood and presented as to meet the legitimate concerns of those Christians who have traditionally opposed the doctrine. Clearly the measure of agreement on this topic was less than on previous subjects. Nevertheless, the dialogue succeeded in elevating a long-standing debate from entrenched contradiction to an open mutual search for truth in respect and Christian love. Its report, *Teaching Authority and Infallibility in the Church*, a volume of 366 pages, appeared in 1980.[15]

From 1979 until 1983 the dialogue engaged in the study of its seventh topic, justification by faith. The dialogue members noted that this subject had been touched upon or alluded to earlier in the dialogue but had never been fully addressed. Since this doctrine played such a prominent role in the development of the Reformation, it required investigation for the improvement of relationships between Roman Catholics and Lutherans. The dialogue group in their common statement declared that they shared the affirmation that the entire hope of justification and salvation rests on Christ Jesus and on the gospel whereby the good news of God's merciful action in Christ is made known. The commission recognized that differences in thought structure play a considerable role in causing tension between Catholic and Lutheran views of justification. Yet it states that in the light of convergences which exist, Lutherans and Catholics can acknowledge the legitimacy of concerns that come to expression in different ways and that theological disagreements about the structures of thought, though serious, need not be church dividing.[16]

After completing its statement on justification in September of 1983, the dialogue turned to the topic of sanctification and the role of the saints. For twenty years this bilateral conversation has contributed to theological scholarship in the pursuit of ecumenical understanding. In its thousands of pages of published work it has helped to change attitudes and relations between Lutherans and Roman Catholics not only in the United States but elsewhere.

During the years of the United States Lutheran–Roman Catholic dialogue, a bilateral on the world level has also been taking place. In June 1965 a Roman Catholic–Lutheran working group was authorized by the Roman Catholic Church and in July 1965 by the Lutheran World Federation. This group decided that theological dialogue between the two communions should be undertaken. One study group was to explore the theology of marriage and the problem of mixed marriages; another was to take up the theme of the gospel and the church. The former topic was finally addressed in the final report of the Roman Catholic–Lutheran–Reformed Study Commission in 1976.[17]

In 1976 the first meeting of the study commission on "The Gospel and the Church" met. The group was not to study the theological controversies of the sixteenth century as such but was to examine the confessional differences in the light of contemporary biblical theology and church history as well as of perspectives opened up by the Second Vatican Council. Seven Roman Catholics and six Lutherans were appointed respectively by the Secretariat for Promoting Christian Unity and the Lutheran World Federation. The World Council of Churches was represented by an observer. The report was completed and released in 1972. Sometimes called the Malta Report, it affirms the authority of the Word of God in and over the church. Polemical misconceptions of the doctrine of justification and sanctification are corrected. Substantial agreements about the sacrificial character of the Eucharist and the real presence of Christ, and in some measure on ministry and order, are stated. The Malta Report recommended the possibility of a mutual recognition of ministries and intercommunion, although four Roman Catholic members expressed reservations on this latter point. The statement listed theological topics that will still need to be addressed: the relation of gospel, church, and faith to the sacraments; the relation of nature and grace, and of Law and Gospel; the magisterium; Mariology; and the papal office.

After publication of the Malta Report, *The Gospel and the Church,* a new commission was set up. The membership was more international, and along with scholars, church authorities and pastors were more strongly represented than in the past. The commission was appointed by the Executive Committee of the Lutheran World Federation and the Secretariat for Promoting Christian Unity. After analyzing the reactions to the Malta Report and contemporary relations between the two communions, topics for the new dialogue were determined. It was decided that three areas not sufficiently discussed in the Malta Report should be taken up: Eucharist, episcopal office, and ways to community.

The English edition of *The Eucharist* was published in 1980. The

German edition had preceded it by two years. The volume contains two appendices: one provides examples of eucharistic liturgies of both churches and from different countries to show how the celebration of the Eucharist is actually conducted in the churches by each side of the dialogue; the other includes six essays by Catholic and Lutheran theologians on important issues. The dialogue commission concluded that agreement was possible on significant issues and unanimously presented the document to the churches for study.

The report *Ways to Community* (English edition 1981, German edition 1980) was issued by the dialogue to provide clarity and a measure of agreement about the goal of unity and concrete steps toward unity. It is a summary of points of agreement rather than a study of previously undiscussed or unresolved problems. The volume reflects a general ecumenical consensus by drawing on the work of the World Council of Churches as well as Roman Catholic and Lutheran statements. It indicates a number of important practical steps that can be taken to promote the ecumenical movement. Included in the volume is "All Under One Christ," the statement on the Augsburg Confession issued by the commission in 1980 to mark the 450th anniversary of this confessional document. The dialogue approved this statement unanimously and declared that it hoped the unanimity expressed here might hasten the hoped-for unity of their churches.

The third study of the bilateral, *The Ministry in the Church* (English edition 1982, German edition 1981) is a technical rather than a pastoral document. It pays special attention to the episcopate. The text recognizes that on both sides the theology of ministry arose in large part out of mutual controversy. The object of the report is to set forth clearly what the two communions have in common regarding the ministry, both in doctrine and in practice, while not ignoring the remaining differences. Although the agreements identified in the understanding of ministry and episcopacy do not remove all differences, the dialogue participants believe that they can have momentous consequences for their churches. The commission urges the churches to consider seriously both their work and the practical implications it raises.

The final topic of the Roman Catholic–Lutheran Joint Commission dealt with models of unity and suggested a process leading to a common office of oversight for the two communions. It is a process that will merit careful consideration in other ecumenical contexts and may be of use not only to Roman Catholics and Lutherans but also to Anglicans. In 1984 the international Lutheran–Roman Catholic dialogue completed its tasks.[18] Within approximately a decade of work it produced significant reports on key issues that had kept Lutheran and Roman Catholic churches separated. No doubt a new chapter of Lutheran–Roman Catholic bilateral conversations will open on the world level after the Seventh Assembly of the Lutheran World Federation in Budapest in 1984.

## LUTHERAN-REFORMED DIALOGUE

Lutheran-Reformed dialogue on the international level originated in 1967 when the Lutheran World Federation and the World Alliance of Reformed Churches set up a joint committee to evaluate the conversations held in Europe and North America. This committee recommended establishment of a permanent committee to further consensus between Lutheran and Reformed churches and to seek ways of achieving a closer working relationship between these two world families. This permanent committee, appointed by the executive committees of the two world bodies, consisted of six members from each side. Its work focused on "concord" as a model of church fellowship, the present relationship between Lutheran and Reformed churches, justification, the implications of the Leuenberg Agreement—an agreement between European Lutheran and Reformed churches—and the role and purpose of confessional families.[19]

In 1984 plans were drawn up between the Lutheran World Federation and the World Alliance of Reformed Churches for an international dialogue to begin in 1985.

Lutheran-Reformed dialogue in the United States was proposed by Dr. James McCord, secretary of the North American area of the World Alliance of Reformed Churches, in 1960. The plans for such a conversation were approved in 1961 by that organization and by the U.S.A. National Committee of the Lutheran World Federation. The dialogue commission consisted of sixteen delegates, six alternates, and three officers of the sponsoring organizations. Included were representatives not affiliated with the two sponsoring bodies: the Lutheran Church—Missouri Synod, the Orthodox Presbyterian Church, and the Christian Reformed Church. The goal of the dialogue was to explore the theological relationships between the Lutheran and the Reformed churches to discover to what extent differences that have divided these communions in the past still constitute obstacles to mutual understanding. After an initial meeting in 1962, four annual consultations took place. The papers and discussion summaries were published as booklets and finally in a single volume entitled *Marburg Revisited*.[20] The dialogue sought to penetrate behind the divisive positions of the sixteenth century to the issues at stake and to rethink those issues in the light of present-day theological scholarship. The dialogue claimed a reaffirmation and fresh discovery of common foundations and evangelical concerns. After studies on the gospel, confession, and Scripture, on Christology and the Lord's Supper, on justification, on Law and Gospel, on creation and redemption, and on ethics, the bilateral concluded that none of the remaining differences should prevent fellowship. The final report asked the churches to enter into discussions looking forward to intercommunion and the fuller recognition of one another's ministries.

None of the constituent churches of the sponsoring confessional organizations took any official action on the dialogue report. However, in 1971 plans were made for a second series of Lutheran-Reformed dialogue. In the time since the end of the earlier dialogue, the Leuenberg Agreement had been reached between Lutheran and Reformed churches in Europe. This had caused considerable interest in the United States. The mandate of the second series was clear: to assess the consensus and the remaining differences in the theology and life of the participating churches as they bear upon the teaching of the gospel in the current situation. The commission was composed of twelve representatives and six alternates. The churches represented were the American Lutheran Church, the Lutheran Church in America, the Lutheran Church—Missouri Synod, the Presbyterian Church in the U.S.A., the United Presbyterian Church, the Christian Reformed Church, the Reformed Church in America, and the United Church of Christ. The group perceived a twofold task: to evaluate the relations between the churches and to assess the consensuses as well as the remaining differences. Between 1972 and 1974 the dialogue discussed the Leuenberg Agreement, identity and identification of the two traditions, the official positions on pulpit and altar fellowship, and an assessment of consensus and remaining differences. This second series did not move beyond the first series and bring about church fellowship, as had been hoped it would. The commission discovered that it had to retreat from its hopes for consensus and give attention to the sources of diversity of theological understanding and to the differences of ecclesiastical life that contributed to the separation between Lutheran and Reformed churches. Two factors contributed to this situation: the cultural and ecclesiastical context had changed since the 1960s and a clear theological consensus claimed by the first series was called into question. This dialogue ended in disappointment. The three representatives from the Lutheran Church—Missouri Synod abstained from signing the final report. The final report declared that the dialogue attempted to express its unity in terms of the Leuenberg Agreement and was unsuccessful. The papers and reports of this second series were never published in a collected form. This series of dialogue painfully demonstrates that not all bilaterals lead to convergence or consensus.

Despite the lack of progress in the second series of dialogue, there was a willingness, especially from the Reformed churches, to renew bilateral conversations with Lutherans. Proposals for a new dialogue were acted on by the Lutheran Council in the U.S.A. and the Caribbean and North American Area Council of the World Alliance of Reformed Churches in 1980. The following year the first meeting of the third series took place. Participating churches included the Association of Evangelical Lutheran Churches, the American Lutheran Church, the Lutheran Church in America, the Lutheran Church—Missouri Synod, the Reformed Church in America, the Presbyterian Church in the U.S.A., the Cumberland Presbyterian Church, and the United Church of Christ. Over a period of three years the dialogue discussed justification, the Lord's Supper, and the ministry. It produced joint statements on these topics and a common statement, entitled "An Invitation to Action." This statement asks the sponsoring churches to take positive action on the results of the dialogue so that the two traditions of the continental Reformation may recognize their significant theological agreement and participate in specific common activities. It mentions fourteen affinities in doctrine and practice of the Lutheran and Reformed traditions. The common statement requests its sponsoring churches, members of the Caribbean and North American Area Council of the World Alliance of Reformed Churches, with the exception of the Cumberland Presbyterian Church, and the Lutheran Council in the U.S.A. to receive the dialogue's report and study it so that it may be widely used in the churches. These churches are called upon to take action at their highest level of authority to enter into a series of recognitions and into common expressions of their life together. The list is perhaps the most extensive suggested by any bilateral conversation. The representatives of the Lutheran Church—Missouri Synod issued a minority report in which the series of recognitions and proposals for common experiences of life were rejected because, in the views of the Missouri Synod participants, a number of substantial issues remain unresolved. Apart from the Lutheran Church—Missouri Synod, all other participating churches in their appropriate conventions or assemblies in 1984 or 1985 thanked the dialogue members for their work and committed themselves to a program of study of the dialogue report, joint statements, and other material looking forward to some possible official acts in 1986. This collection of texts, entitled *An Invitation to Action,* was sent to all clergy of the sponsoring churches in 1984.[21]

Within the last twenty years, ecumenical dialogues or bilateral conversations have been an effective tool for ecumenical advance between certain churches. They have been able to put centuries-old conflicts into a new light and thus have enabled churches in varying degrees to move beyond these controversies. The dialogues of the future will continue to offer new hopes, although the most challenging aspect of dialogues in the immediate future is to see that they are taken seriously by the churches that called for them in the first place.

## NOTES

1. See Nils Ehrenström and Günther Gassmann, *Confessions in Dialogue,* Faith and Order Paper 74, 3d ed., rev. and enlarged (Geneva: World Council of Churches, 1975), 10.

2. Ibid.

3. Harding Meyer and Lukas Vischer, eds., *Growth in Agreement: Reports and Agreed Statements of Ecumenical Conversations on a World Level* (New York and Ramsey: Paulist Press, 1984).

4. See Herbert J. Ryan, S.J., and J. Robert Wright, eds., *Episcopalians and Roman Catholics: Can They Ever Get Together?* (Denville, N.J.: Dimension Books, 1972).

5. *The Final Report: Anglican–Roman Catholic International Commission* (Cincinnati: Forward Movement Publications, 1982; Washington, D.C.: Office of Publishing Services, U.S. Catholic Conference, 1982).

6. Meyer and Vischer, eds., *Growth in Agreement,* 13–34.

7. *Lutheran-Episcopal Dialogue: A Progress Report* (Cincinnati: Forward Movement Publications, 1973).

8. *Lutheran-Episcopal Dialogue: The Report of the Lutheran-Episcopal Dialogue: Second Series 1976–1980* (Cincinnati: Forward Movement Publications, 1981).

9. See *The Lutheran-Episcopal Agreement: Commentary and Guidelines* (New York: Division for World Mission and Ecumenism, Lutheran Church in America, 1983).

10. *Anglican-Lutheran Dialogue: The Report of the Anglican-Lutheran European Regional Commission* (London: S.P.C.K., 1983).

11. *Anglican-Lutheran Relations: Report—Anglican Joint Working Group* (London: Anglican Consultative Council, 1983; Geneva: Lutheran World Federation, 1983).

12. In 1973 a combined report of *Lutherans and Roman Catholics in Dialogue, Vols. I–III* was issued: Paul C. Empie and T. Austin Murphy, eds., *Lutherans and Catholics in Dialogue I–III* (Minneapolis: Augsburg Publishing House, 1973).

13. Paul C. Empie and T. Austin Murphy, eds., *Lutherans and Catholics in Dialogue IV: Eucharist and Ministry* (New York: U.S.A. National Committee of Lutheran World Federation, 1970; Washington, D.C.: Bishops' Committee for Ecumenical and Interreligious Affairs, 1970).

14. Paul C. Empie and T. Austin Murphy, eds., *Lutherans and Catholics in Dialogue V: Papal Primacy and the Universal Church* (Minneapolis: Augsburg Publishing House, 1974).

15. Paul C. Empie, T. Austin Murphy, and Joseph A. Burgess, eds., *Lutherans and Catholics in Dialogue VI: Teaching Authority and Infallibility in the Church* (Minneapolis: Augsburg Publishing House, 1980).

16. H. George Anderson, T. Austin Murphy, and Joseph A. Burgess, eds., *Lutherans and Catholics in Dialogue VII: Justification by Faith* (Minneapolis: Augsburg Publishing House, 1985).

17. Meyer and Vischer, eds., *Growth in Agreement,* 277–306.

18. The published reports of the international Lutheran-Roman Catholic

dialogue can be found in Meyer and Vischer, eds., *Growth in Agreement,* 167–275.

19. The Leuenberg Agreement is included in the latest report of Lutheran-Reformed Dialogue in the United States, pp. 61–74. See footnote 21.

20. Paul C. Empie and James I. McCord, eds., *Marburg Revisited: A Re-examination of Lutheran and Reformed Traditions* (Minneapolis: Augsburg Publishing House, 1966).

21. James E. Andrews and Joseph A. Burgess, eds., *An Invitation to Action: The Lutheran-Reformed Dialogue, Series III* (Philadelphia: Fortress Press, 1984).

# 6

# ECUMENISM
# TODAY

This chapter will examine how the ecumenical movement has made its impact felt within several Christian communions. In each case we will review documents produced by specific churches that speak to the relation of that particular church to ecumenism. Admittedly, official church documents do not always furnish an accurate reflection of where the membership is or of the direction in which it wishes to go. For the communions reflected here, however, there appears to be ample support for the contention that these statements cited, at either the national or the international level, are accurate litmus tests of how ecumenism is influencing these churches. We will begin with the Anglican communion and more specifically with the Episcopal Church, U.S.A.

Any history of the church in the twentieth century makes clear the commitment of Anglicans to the ecumenical movement. Anglican churches and their members have played key roles in international, national, and regional ecumenical efforts throughout this century. One specific example of this involvement is the triennial ecumenical study carried on by the Episcopal Church, U.S.A., between 1976 and 1979. Although conducted some nine years ago in a different ecumenical context from the mid-1980s, it is still an important articulation of how one church views its ecumenical responsibilities. A major event in the study was a national ecumenical consultation sponsored by the Episcopal Church, U.S.A., in November 1978 near Detroit. The papers delivered at this consultation, along with its report, were published in 1979 in a volume edited by J. Robert Wright, entitled *A Communion of Communions: One Eucharistic Fellowship.*[1] This volume has three purposes: (1) to state the ecumenical goals toward which the Episcopal Church, U.S.A., intends to move, (2) to assess the Episcopal Church's general ecumenical posture, and (3) to restate those essentials to which the Anglicans are committed. An overview of the report of this study, the so-called Detroit Report, demonstrates how one church relates to the ecumenical movement.[2]

The Detroit Report opens with a strong statement that the Lord of the church through Scripture, the tradition of the church, the needs of humankind, and the ecumenical movement calls his church to make visible the unity he has given to the church. With other churches of the Anglican communion, the Episcopal Church, U.S.A., is committed to the ecumenical movement and to the goal of visible unity. Visible unity is defined by the Detroit Report as one eucharistic fellowship, "a communion of communions, based upon a mutual recognition of catholicity." In this communion of communions, churches recognize one another's members and ministers, share eucharistic fellowship, acknowledge membership in the church catholic throughout time and space, engage in a common proclamation of the gospel, and share a mutual trust and dedication to the needs of the world. Common assemblies of churches are envisioned. The final shape of the collegiality, conciliarity, authority, and primacy is not described, but there is a recognition that the particular traditions of each communion should be maintained and developed for the enrichment of the whole church. Visible unity will require long and steady growth, taken in steps. Episcopalians in this process are called upon to understand anew the dynamic tension among the apostolic, catholic, and reformed aspects of their character.

In view of all this, the document calls for specific action. Theological reflection is encouraged in dioceses, parishes, theological seminaries, and the various groups within the church called to common prayer and study. A series of recommendations is offered asking for considerable study and coordination between Episcopalians and Roman Catholics based on the progress of that dialogue up to 1978. Other recommendations follow that deal with the work of the Consultation on Church Union (COCU) and ask for study of the COCU materials. It is suggested that a procedure be developed from this study to aid in responding to the emerging theological consensus in the bilateral conversations of the Episcopal Church, U.S.A., with the

Orthodox, Roman Catholic, and Lutheran churches. Finally in this section, recommendations speak of the need for the sharing of ecumenical information within the Anglican communion and especially more study of the report of the Anglican-Orthodox joint commission.

Following the initial subsection on visible unity, the report turns to spiritual ecumenism, the life of prayer and worship. It suggests that the ecumenical agreements reached by Episcopalians must be tested by Anglican spirituality. This spiritual discernment requires knowledge and appreciation of how the other churches involved in agreements educate their members in the life of prayer through public worship and private devotion. Theological agreements need to be tested by the appreciation and experience of the spiritual treasures of the other Christian traditions. Spiritual ecumenism is endorsed as that change of heart toward Christians of other traditions which prompts divided Christians to receive from one another such gifts as biblical interpretation, liturgies, prayers, hymns, and spiritual exercises. The report speaks of the urgency for such spiritual ecumenism in today's world. After a series of perceptions on this topic come a number of recommendations, including the proposal for a statement on eucharistic practice that would (1) acknowledge the Sacrament of the Lord's Supper as a means to unity and not just a sign of unity and (2) supply a standard for those persons of other churches who desire to receive Holy Communion in Episcopal churches.

The third subsection of the first part of the report is devoted to partnership: the apostolate to the world. It states that commitment to the gospel requires that the Episcopal Church, U.S.A., and those other churches with which it is in dialogue find ways to proclaim by word and example the good news, to seek and serve Christ in all persons, and to strive for justice and peace among all people with respect for the dignity of every human being. Detailed recommendations call for common Christian study and action on social issues and a reaffirmation of the Lund Principle as an effective means of stewardship in the use of talents and resources.

The second major portion of the Detroit Report addresses principles of unity. Although the gospel calls Christians to unity in the church, this fellowship is visibly divided, its purpose obscured, its mission impeded, and its witness weakened. The Episcopal Church,

U.S.A., actively seeks unity on the basis of the vision of the Chicago-Lambeth Quadrilateral of 1886 and 1888, a nineteenth-century document that sought Christian unity based on the Holy Scriptures, the ecumenical creeds, the two sacraments of Baptism and the Lord's Supper, and the historic episcopate. The Detroit Report recognizes this basis, but also speaks of the need to discover new patterns of Christian unity. Reaffirming the spirit of the Quadrilateral, it proposes new affirmations of these principles for ecumenical reunion in the present. These affirmations, four in number, describe the essentials for Christian unity as (1) mutual recognition of Scriptures, (2) mutual recognition of the ancient creeds, (3) mutual recognition of the church as the sacrament of God's presence to the world and as a sign of the Kingdom, and (4) mutual recognition of apostolicity as evidenced in continuity with the teaching, the ministry, and the mission of the apostles. Refinements of the points of the Lambeth Quadrilateral contained in the Detroit Report are of notable significance, reflecting great ecumenical sensitivity, and are worthy of careful study.[3] Building on the Lambeth Quadrilateral, these principles increase the possibility of ecumenical advancement by applying the conclusions of biblical and historical scholarship in this century.

The final subsection of the document offers analysis and recommendations regarding each of the conversations in which the Episcopal Church is engaged. This is the part of the report most affected by the passage of time, since its observations are based on circumstances that prevailed in 1978. Still, in many ways, it is a useful analysis and indicator of the constant issues of the ecumenical agenda. The Consultation on Church Union, with its document *In Quest of a Church of Christ Uniting,* is reviewed first. Then the Anglican-Orthodox theological consultation is discussed. Its value is stressed despite the fact that the ordination of women by the Episcopal Church has caused difficulties for the dialogue. The Lutheran-Episcopal dialogue is affirmed. Study of the Pullach Report and the first series of Lutheran-Episcopal dialogue is recommended. The need for further work is required concerning eucharistic sharing, including the request for eucharistic sharing by participants in several series of dialogue. Major attention is given to the Anglican–Roman Catholic consultation. It is clear that in 1978 this bilateral had a high priority for the Episcopal Church. There are certainly obvious reasons why this would be the case. The major difficulty in Anglican and Roman Catholic relationships is that of authority, which relates also to the question of the ordination of women to the diaconate and priesthood. The complementarity of the Episcopal Church's participation in the Consultation on Church Union, Lutheran dialogue, and Roman Catholic dialogue is insisted upon. All of these ecumenical conversations seek to promote the integral catholicity of Christ's church. In spite of difficulties, the Detroit Report declares that it expects Anglican–Roman Catholic dialogue to produce a mutual statement of common faith sufficient to permit reconciliation of Anglican and Roman Catholic ordained ministers, which would in turn make possible a full sacramental sharing between the two churches.

Like all theological documents, the Detroit Report is time conditioned. It speaks out of a particular context. Some of the specific items addressed have developed quite differently from what anyone would have suspected even in 1978. Probably few at the Detroit consultation would have thought that the Lutheran-Episcopal Agreement was only four years away. In other regards the analysis of the report has been impressively accurate. The Detroit Report gives clear evidence of the influence of the ecumenical movement on one church. It reveals how the Episcopal Church, U.S.A., has acquired an ecumenical vision of the type that has allowed it to be faithful to its past, aware of its present, and open to a future which it recognizes will have both continuities and discontinuities with its past and present. A more recent document displays this same kind of ecumenical commitment with the world Anglican communion. Entitled *Steps Towards Unity*, it was produced in 1984 by the Anglican Consultative Council, headquartered in London.[4]

*Steps Towards Unity* opens with a survey of the present world scene of disunities and the impressive but complex activity of theological dialogue and notes the involvement of the Anglican communion both in bilateral and multilateral conversations. In 1984, four international conversations were before the churches of the Anglican communion for consideration. A significant portion of the entire document is given to *Baptism, Eucharist and Ministry* and the questions being addressed to the churches by the World Council of Churches Commission on Faith and Order. Use of *Baptism, Eucharist and Ministry* is encouraged within the Anglican Consultative Council. The distinction is drawn between the official response to *Baptism, Eucharist and Ministry* and the process of reception of the document by the whole people of God. Comments are then made on the work of the Anglican–Roman Catholic International Commission, particularly the present stage of study and official response to the final report of ARCIC. Guidelines are offered to the Provinces of the Anglican Communion for their study of whether the final report is consonant in substance with the faith of Anglicans and whether it offers a sufficient basis for the next concrete step toward reconciliation. Then more briefly the document examines Anglican-Orthodox joint doctrinal discussions and Anglican–Oriental Orthodox relations. More extensive attention is given to Anglican-Lutheran relations. This section reviews the work of international and selected national or regional dialogues. It describes the work accomplished by the international Anglican-Lutheran Joint Working Group at the end of 1983 and endorses the model of "interim eucharistic sharing" developed in the United States. The text turns next to the report of the Anglican-Reformed International Commission, completed in 1984. This report, while addressing some of the obstacles that have hindered Anglican-Reformed union proposals and schemes not only helps these churches to overcome these obstacles but has significance for a wider context. The dialogue report is less specialized and less condensed in style than the Anglican–Roman Catholic International Commission's final report or *Baptism, Eucharist and Ministry.* Appended to it are questions suitable for discussion at the local level. The Provinces of the Anglican Communion are asked to give these questions serious study. The final part of *Steps Toward Unity* addresses the important concept of unity by stages. This portion builds on a 1981 report on the same subject but moves beyond it in view of the different situation three years later. It distinguishes four aims and objectives of dialogues: fellowship in faith and mission, limited eucharistic sharing, full communion, and organic union. These different goals and stages of unity look different in the context of the different dialogues. All the dialogues have made significant clarifications of the process of uniting by stages and of the terms used. Nevertheless more work needs to be done; for example, it is not now fully known what the terms "full communion" and "organic union" mean or how they differ, if in fact they do. The final report of the Anglican–Roman Catholic International Commission seems to make no distinction. The conclusion of this document from the Anglican Consultative Council raises the question of the experience and recovery of unity locally. This must be done pastorally. Local experience can give personal and corporate reality, and meaning, to the wider search for unity which sometimes is in danger of being abstract and impersonal. On the other hand local unity can be partial and even sectarian without regard to the wider unity of the church.

We will next turn to one Lutheran church to investigate how the ecumenical movement has been a major force in its life. As the result of a merger of four Lutheran churches, the Lutheran Church in America came into being in 1963. All of the predecessor bodies of the Lutheran Church in America were committed, in varying degrees, to the ecumenical movement. They supplied leadership and resources to Faith and Order and Life and Work as well as to the developing councils of churches.[5] This commitment was written into the constitution of the new church in 1962. The constitution held before this church not only the unification of all Lutherans but the concept of Christian unity as well.[6] In its early history, the Lutheran Church in America began to live out in obvious ways this understanding of its ecumenical role. It took an active part in ecumenical organizations and in the bilateral conversations that were beginning to take place in the 1960s. Based on a long history of ecumenical involvement, all arenas of the life of the Lutheran Church in America participated in varying degrees in ecumenical activities. Ecumenical activity on the national level was focused in, although not monopolized by, the then Office of the President. Presidents Franklin C. Fry and Robert J. Marshall played key ecumenical roles. Some ecumenical functions were discharged by Dr. Malvin H. Lundeen and Dr. George F. Harkins, who served as Secretaries of the Lutheran Church in America. In 1972, the church underwent a structural reorganization and the Division for World Mission and Ecumenism was formed. For the first time, ecumenism had a place in the structures of the church in addition to the Office of the President. But while a specific structural locus for ecumenism must be applauded, the exact choice cannot be. Any office of ecumenism needs direct contact with the chief executive office of the church. This is especially true in the Lutheran Church in America in view of the constitutional responsibilities of the Office of the President, which in 1980 became the Office of the Bishop. Also in the new division, ecumenism all too often played a secondary role, its central thrust of unity being ignored. Not until 1979, following the 1978 election of James R. Crumley, Jr., as president (the title changing to bishop after 1980) was a staff position established in the Division to handle ecumenical responsibilities. In 1979 the position of Director for Ecumenical Relations was introduced as part of the Division, but with direct administrative responsibility to the bishop. The Department for Ecumenical Relations and the position of Assistant Director for Ecumenical Relations were created in 1982. In spite of the sluggishness of these developments, the Division for World Mission and Ecumenism deserves credit for undertaking a consultation on ecumenism in 1981. The purpose of this gathering, which brought together most of the individuals in the Lutheran Church in America who had ecumenical responsibilities on the national and international levels, was to examine the ecumenical goals and program of the church. Unexpectedly at the end of the consultation, the idea of developing an official position for the Lutheran Church in America on its ecumenical commitment came into being. This had not been part of the original plan. Time was short before the next biennial convention of the church which was scheduled to meet in Louisville in September 1982. Nevertheless, a process was quickly put in place and a drafting committee appointed. In the spring of 1982 the Division for World Mission and Ecumenism transmitted the draft of a statement on ecumenism to the convention for action. In September 1982, at its Eleventh Biennial Convention, the Lutheran Church in America enthusiastically adopted *Ecumenism: A Lutheran Commitment* as an official position of the church.[7] Much in the document had been implicit in the Lutheran Church in America and its predecessor bodies, but now this church was making explicit its views of, and commitment to, ecumenism. Here was a statement of this church's ecumenical heritage and a vision for its ecumenical future.

*Ecumenism: A Lutheran Commitment* is divided into a preface and six major sections. The preface states, "This unity is God's gift in the life of the Church under Christ and the Spirit. Ecumenism is the experience and on-going task of expressing this unity." The first section deals with scriptural, confessional, and constitutional foundations. It declares that the vision of the Lutheran Church in America as an ecumenical church is dependent on an understanding of Scripture and the Lutheran Confessions which is also found in the constitution of this church. Then follows an overview of New Testament teaching on unity, a unity in diversity pictured realistically within the context of human inclinations against unity and fellowship. The Lutheran Confessions are seen as products of an effort at evangelical reform, which, contrary to its intention, resulted in divisions within the Western church. They are viewed as evangelical writings, stressing justification by grace through faith, concerned for the oneness of the church, the preservation of the catholic heritage, and the renewal of the whole church. Indebted to recent scholarship, the statement presents the Confessions, not as denominational charters, but as ecumenical proposals to the entire church. This is true of its interpretation of the Augsburg Confession, especially Article 7, which according to the statement has as its underlying intention, not the adoption of the Lutheran reforms by others, but their recognition as legitimately Christian. The ecumenical potential of the Confessions is affirmed. Because the Confessions insist that agreement in the gospel suffices for Christian unity, Lutherans are free to enter into church fellowship without insisting on doctrinal or ecclesiastical uniformity. When there is consensus on the gospel, there can be room for living and experiencing fellowship within the context of seeking larger theological agreement. This view is a new emphasis within Lutheranism and would probably not receive unanimous endorsement within world Lutheranism. Its proponents are convinced that it is faithful to the original intention of the Lutheran Reformers. *Ecumenism: A Lutheran Commitment* then explains how the vision of a larger wholeness to Christianity expressed in the Scriptures and the Lutheran Confessions finds expression in the constitution of the Lutheran Church in America. The ecumenical statement moves from the constitutional document to make explicit a new stress: Christian unity may be sought even while hoping for Lutheran unification. It states clearly that the fulfillment of Lutheran unification is not to be a condition for taking steps toward Christian unity.

The second section describes the evangelical, catholic, and ecumenical stance of the Lutheran Church in America. This church sees itself as a manifestation of the church evangelical, catholic, and ecumenical. It understands "evangelical" to mean centered in the gospel which is the unconditional promise of God, who in Christ justified the ungodly by grace through faith apart from works. "Catholic" means to be centered in the apostolic faith and its credal, doctrinal articulation for the entire world. This involves the recognition of the church as a community, rooted in the Christ event, extending through time. "Ecumenical" means to be centered in the oneness that comes from God. It involves participation in the ecumenical movement. This section closes with a pledge by the Lutheran Church in America to affirm its kinship and to demonstrate its unity with all those who are evangelical and catholic in the church.

The next part of the document sketches the ecumenical involvements of the Lutheran Church in America since 1962. It shows how the church was active in ecumenism between 1962 and 1982, tracing developments in councils, on the global scene, in the Roman Catholic Church, in ecumenical dialogues, and in local ecumenism. The great importance of this last area is underscored. More attention must be given to local ecumenism. The Lutheran Church in America has much to learn from and to offer to local ecumenism.

The fourth segment looks toward the future of ecumenical relations. The Lutheran Church in America professes that it is ready to commit itself more fully to the ecumenical implications of its faith and life. Fourteen insights are given to supply guidance. Among the more important are the following:

- The centrality of the gospel, affirmed in the Lutheran Confessions, allows for considerable variety in many aspects of ecclesial life and organization, doctrinal expression, and ethical assertions.
- Ecumenism embodies all those churches which confess the triune God. This includes not only Anglicans, Reformed, and Roman Catholics but also Orthodox, Methodists, Baptists, Conservative Evangelicals, and Pentecostals.

- Progress in one area of ecumenism must not be seen as competitive with advancement in another.
- The vision of unity shared by the World Council of Churches is affirmed for the present stage of the ecumenical movement.
- The Lutheran Confessions are an ecumenical resource, to be appreciated for their liberating effect.
- Where there is agreement in the gospel, forms of eucharistic hospitality may take place and become part of the experience that moves churches toward fuller Christian unity. This position, developed in the dialogues, is a new emphasis in contrast to the older Lutheran view of complete doctrinal consensus before any altar fellowship.
- The bilateral and multilateral dialogues are encouraged.
- The statement is made that God may always have surprises for his people that are beyond human comprehension.

The conclusion, section five, in the biblical image of the grain of wheat falling to the earth and dying, declares that in ecclesiology, divisions and structures may well need to die if greater unity, as God wills, is to come. No church may be exalted in contrast to the truth of the gospel and the unity God wills.

*Ecumenism: A Lutheran Commitment* closes with a number of commitments made by the Lutheran Church in America. These include membership in ecumenical organizations, a reaffirmation of the desire for Lutheran unity, acknowledgment of its oneness in faith with all churches that accept the unaltered Augsburg Confession and the Small Catechism of Luther, a reaffirmation to cooperative ministry and mission with other churches and ecumenical agencies, invitations to its biennial convention of ecumenical observers, and commitment to prompt action on ecumenical documents requiring official action by churches. Ecumenical commitment to the unity of the church is seen as among the highest priorities of the Lutheran Church in America under the proclamation of the gospel.

This official position of the Lutheran Church in America has been regarded within world Lutheranism and by other Christian churches as an extremely helpful resource for ecumenical advance. It allows the Lutheran Church in America to be faithful to its scriptural and confessional roots and to be free with integrity to move in the present ecumenical context to closer expressions of unity with Lutherans and other Christians. One of the pressing challenges and opportunities before this church is to share this ecumenical articulation and stance within the process of the formation of a new Lutheran church in the United States so that this new church is not less ecumenical but at least as ecumenical as the Lutheran Church in America in 1984.

Now we turn to another Christian communion to examine the impact of the ecumenical movement. It has been observed in earlier chapters that Orthodox churches have been actively involved in the ecumenical movement for many years. Therefore it is not surprising to find attention given to this topic within Orthodox churches. Many examples could be given. Here we will examine a statement prepared by the Orthodox Church in America entitled *Christian Unity and Ecumenism.* The document contains a clear message of ecumenical involvement and expresses a number of concerns that would be shared by the Orthodox generally. The Orthodox Church in America's origins lie in the eighteenth century in the mission work of the Russian Orthodox Church. In 1970 this church was granted complete self-government by the Russian Orthodox Church. Its statement on ecumenism is an encyclical letter of the synod of Bishops of the Orthodox Church in America, approved in 1973.[8] Although some twelve years old, the document is probably still representative of Orthodox views of the ecumenical movement.

The encyclical letter opens with a statement of explanation of the participation of the Orthodox Church in the ecumenical movement. The Orthodox have been involved in this genuine, although imperfect search for the unity of all in Christ because of the injunctions of Scripture for the unity of the church. "Ecumenism" and "ecumenical movement" are defined as "all forms of activity directed to reunion of divided Christians in the one Church of Christ." Concern is expressed that the ecumenical movement itself has changed radically and that Orthodox positions on the ecumenical movement have shifted.

The first major section of the letter describes the unity of the church. Any unity not rooted in God through Christ and the Holy Spirit is not Christian unity. Christ, being God and man, is the center and uniting power of the church. This unity is a unity in truth. There is no Christian unity outside the truth, for outside the truth there is no church, no salvation, and no eternal life. This truth of God is unchanging and eternal. Christ declared that his teachings will never change. He promised the Holy Spirit to his believers. The Holy Spirit came to the apostles so they could teach what Christ had taught. The apostles did not fashion their own doctrines but proclaimed the teachings of Christ. This doctrinal truth of the apostolic church is the eternal and unchanging truth of God himself. It abides in the church and is handed down from time to time and from place to place in the Holy Tradition. Therefore the only possible unity for Christians is the unity of faith to which the apostles, saints, and councils have witnessed. The Holy Tradition is the entire spiritual treasury given by God in Christ and the Spirit to all believers in all times and places. The creative task of individual Christians and Christian communities is to realize the Christian faith with all possible depth and fullness, and to transmit it. This unity in truth is also a unity in love and holiness, for love and holiness are living expressions and perfections of truth. Divine holiness is the fundamental basis for genuine Christian unity and the highest expression of this holiness is love. The commandments of God given in Christ and fulfilled in love include the virtues and fruits of Spirit which do not change. Genuine Christian unity, thus, is possible only where believers are one in Christ and the Holy Spirit, fully united in truth, love, and holiness of God. This unity is possible only in that church which continues to proclaim the revelation of God in its fullness, not only in its doctrines and morals but in the whole order of spiritual, sacramental, and hierarchical church life as established in the apostolic Christian community. The Orthodox Church is confessed to be the true church, but corporate and personal failings of its members are acknowledged. Nationalism and ethnicism have often obscured the divine mission of the church. Nevertheless there can only be one church and into this church all must enter to live in communion with God, with each other, and with all creation.

The second major division of the letter deals with the ecumenical movement today. The Orthodox Church has always taken part in this movement on the basis of its fundamental self-understanding. Even if other participants in the ecumenical movement did not share these

Orthodox convictions, they were respected. Today according to this encyclical letter there is a crisis of spirit and orientation in the ecumenical movement. The movement is being confronted by several dangers. There is a trend to a consistent, confessional, doctrinal, and historical relativism. In this view the church is simply a human society. Everything essentially changes in history. Historical relativism says that it is not merely accidental forms of faith that are different, but that the very faith itself can take overtly contradictory forms. Thus the ecumenical movement is no longer the common search for truth, but an attempt to discover and to manifest the minimum of Christian beliefs. All essential differences are allowed. There is also the danger of secularism which is one of the major roots of doctrinal relativism. Some believe that secular activity will bring about the unity of Christians and manifest the unity of the church to the world. In addition there is evident in many ecumenical activities a conscious choice of certain social, political, and economic policies and actions, which it is claimed are the only ones consistent with the Christian faith. Finally there is the danger of false methods of union. All doctrinal, ethical, and sacramental compromises that alter the hierarchical order of the church in and through which the continuity and identity of the church of Christ is realized in space and time are rejected. Eucharistic sharing as a means of achieving Christian unity is not acceptable. The letter records deep disagreement with attempts to transform ecumenism itself into a kind of universal church, uniting persons and groups on the basis of its own conditions rather than on the basis of the absolute, eternal, and unchanging conditions of the gospel.

The final portion of the document concerns Orthodox participation in the ecumenical movement. This participation is reaffirmed, providing that certain conditions are met. These include the denial of error wherever it is found. Whatever is contrary to the Scriptures and Holy Tradition must be refused. Whatever conforms to the faith and life of the Orthodox Church in non-Orthodox communions must be accepted as a basis for positive meeting and cooperation. All who have faith in Christ and have preserved elements of Orthodox Christianity are to be recognized as fellow Christians. The genuine ecumenical movement is to work toward the goal of organic Christian unity. It is uncertain that it can be achieved by Christians on this earth. The achievement of Christian unity insofar as it depends on Orthodox Christians requires the preservation and strengthening of the consensus of opinion and action of the Orthodox in ecumenical affairs. Certain areas of ecumenical cooperation are listed, including common witness of faith in God, common efforts of serving those in need, common witness of the Christian ideal of the human person, and common work to achieve Christian unity in the truth and love of God with an open atmosphere in which opinions are expressed without coercion or pressure. The letter concludes with a plea for all to walk the narrow path of Christ and to follow an ecumenical plan which alone, however slow and painful, can lead to the divine unity given by God to the one, holy, catholic and apostolic church. It is a useful document for all who wish to understand better the basis of Orthodox participation in the ecumenical movement and the contributions and concerns they carry with their involvement.

Roman Catholic interest and involvement on a personal basis in the ecumenical movement are both of long standing. Officially, however, the Roman Catholic Church separated itself for many years from the ecumenical movement. As we observed in chapter 2, the official position of the Roman Catholic Church only changed in the pontificate of Pope John XXIII (1958–1963). Under his leadership the Roman Catholic Church entered and accepted the one ecumenical movement of this century. The reversal of earlier policy is seen most dramatically in the Second Vatican Council of 1962–65. The new attitude of the Roman Catholic Church toward ecumenism is reflected in many aspects of Vatican II and the documents it produced. Perhaps nowhere can this attitude be detected more clearly than in the texts dealing with the church and ecumenism. For convenience we will survey the Decree on Ecumenism, a conciliar document that indicates how the ecumenical movement made its influence felt on Catholic teaching.

On 21 November 1964, at the close of the third session of the Second Vatican Council, Pope Paul VI together with the Council promulgated the Decree on Ecumenism, *Unitas Redintegratio,* along with the Dogmatic Constitution of the Church and the Decree on Eastern Catholic Churches. The Council had earlier approved the

Decree on Ecumenism—2,137 votes in favor and 11 against. In the twenty years since it was issued, the decree has been a mandate and source of guidance for Roman Catholics in the ecumenical movement. It is impossible to understand the present position of the Roman Catholic Church toward ecumenism apart from the Decree on Ecumenism.[9]

The idea for one conciliar document on church unity came about in 1962. Earlier that year Vatican II had struggled with two or three documents dealing with unity, finally voting in December in favor of one document, at least in part because of the lack of coordination of the schemata already prepared. This vote gave birth to the document that became known as the Decree on Ecumenism. During the second session of the Council in November of 1963, a new draft of the text was debated and overwhelmingly approved as a basis for further discussion. Comments on the text suggested that some passages were too cautious and conservative. Pleasantly surprised, the Secretariat for Promoting Christian Unity, under the leadership of Cardinal Bea, supplied a bolder, new draft for the third session. There was no discussion, only voting on the text during this session. Some twenty-nine textual changes were made and reported back to the Council on 10 through 14 November 1964. On 29 November the pope introduced nineteen suggestions for greater clarity. With one exception dealing with the use of Scripture, all were minor alterations. On 21 November 1964 the Council voted its approval of the entire text. It is important to note that the Decree on Ecumenism was proclaimed only after the Council had indicated its teaching on the church. The relationship of these two topics should be underscored. The Decree on Ecumenism needs to be seen according to its own self-understanding in the light of three facts of history: (1) Christ founded one church, and this church is the church catholic, (2) from its beginning, rifts and dissensions appeared and large communities became separated from full communion with this church, and (3) in recent times a Christian movement has appeared that aims at the reconciliation of all Christians in the unity of the one and only church of Christ.

The Decree on Ecumenism should be viewed neither as a handbook of ecumenical theology nor as a historical discussion of divisions in the church. It is primarily a pastoral document. Here the

Roman Catholic Church formulates its present involvement in the ecumenical movement and directs Catholics to respond to the call of Christ and to the grace of the Spirit for the restoration of unity among separated Christians. The conciliar document is not the declaration of a static position but a charter for involvement in a movement. If at points the text reflects a lack of clarity, it may be because the churches, and the ecumenical movement itself, are involved in a pilgrimage whose direction is not completely clear at every point.

The Decree on Ecumenism in its first chapter indicates the Roman Catholic principles of ecumenism by presenting the Roman Catholic Church's understanding of its own unity centered in the office of Peter. The church is God's only flock. Its unity is a sacred mystery whose highest exemplar and source is the unity in the Trinity of Persons. It then continues by describing the relationship to the Roman Catholic Church of separated brethren and their communities. This relationship should be one of respect and affection. Both sides are to blame for divisions. The chapter ends with suggestions to Roman Catholics as to how, under the guidance of their bishops, they can take an active role in the work of ecumenism. They should promote justice and truth, concord and collaboration, as well as love and unity. Little by little, obstacles to perfect ecclesiastical communion will be overcome.

Chapter 2 of the document is concerned with the practice of ecumenism. Here the whole church of faithful and clergy is to be involved. Church renewal has notable ecumenical importance. This renewal takes place in various spheres of the church's life: in biblical study, the liturgical movement, the preaching of the word, and social teaching. Ecumenism requires the continual reformation of the church itself and the constant interior conversion of each believer. The ecumenical movement calls for a change of heart and holiness of life, for private and public prayer for unity, and for occasional joint worship of Roman Catholics and their brothers and sisters in Christ. Worship in common is not to be considered as a means to be used indiscriminately for the restoration of unity among Christians. Mutual understanding will develop from ecumenical dialogue, ecumenically informed theological study, and joint study of the Scripture. A united witness before the world through cooperative action, especially in social matters, is to be encouraged and will express the common bonds that unite Christians to one another and to Christ.

Chapter 3 of the document takes up ecumenical relations in view of the two main divisions that occurred in the Christian family: those divisions which took place in the East and those in the West. In regard to the former, attention must be given to the special features of the origin and growth that caused differences in mentality and historical development with the West. Eastern liturgical and monastic traditions and their disciplines should be respected by Roman Catholics, for these things contribute to the richness of the church and its mission. The principle of legitimate diversity must be respected, especially as it relates to the theological developments of the Eastern churches. Possible and recommended means of restoring unity include prayer, dialogue, and cooperation in pastoral work. Common worship with Eastern churches, in suitable circumstances, is encouraged. The third chapter then turns to divisions in the West and speaks of separated churches and ecclesial communities. The Decree on Ecumenism acknowledges that there are serious differences in faith and government between these churches and communities and the Roman Catholic Church. Nevertheless the document offers helps for the establishment of contacts and the development of relations. Points of agreement on the centrality of Christ, the love and reverence of Scripture, the practice of baptism, the celebration of the Lord's Supper, and witness to the gospel are areas for contacts. The Decree also notes that many of these points are also places of disagreement between Roman Catholics and their brothers and sisters in Christ. The conclusion of the Decree on Ecumenism is a plea for God's blessings on the ecumenical movement and its continuing guidance under his Spirit.

With this remarkable document, the Roman Catholic Church officially entered into the one ecumenical movement according to its own principles and set before its members guidelines, helps, and methods by which they too could respond to the grace of this call. Wisely, the Decree on Ecumenism did not attempt to define ecumenism in a static manner but only provisionally to describe the situation in the 1960s and to offer suggestions to meet this situation. The Second Vatican Council realized that the ecumenical movement was in an initial stage, and the Roman Catholic Church should not be bound too rigorously to changing circumstances.

This chapter has endeavored to document how various Christian traditions have responded to the ecumenical movement. By means of significant documents we have seen how the churches have reacted in the 1970s and 1980s to the challenges and hopes of the movement toward unity. Our remaining question is where does this movement, under God's Spirit, lead the churches in the years beyond the mid-1980s.

## NOTES

1. J. Robert Wright, ed., *A Communion of Communions: One Eucharistic Fellowship* (New York: The Seabury Press, 1979).

2. Ibid., 3–29.

3. Ibid., 16–17.

4. *Steps Toward Unity* (London: Anglican Consultative Council, 1984).

5. E. Theodore Bachmann, *The Ecumenical Involvement of the LCA Predecessor Bodies,* rev. 2d ed. (New York: Division for World Mission and Ecumenism, Lutheran Church in America, 1983).

6. Constitution, Lutheran Church in America, Articles II; IV,2; V,1.

7. *Ecumenism: A Lutheran Commitment* (New York: Lutheran Church in America, 1982).

8. *Christian Unity and Ecumenism* in *Documents of the Orthodox Church in America* (New York: Holy Synod of the Orthodox Church in America, 1973).

9. Austin P. Flannery, ed., *Documents of Vatican II* (Grand Rapids: Wm. B. Eerdmans Publishing Co., 1975), 452–78.

# 7

# ECUMENISM— ITS PROMISE FOR THE FUTURE

Chapter 6 traced how the ecumenical movement has already influenced several major Christian traditions. The ecumenical movement has changed relationships between churches. The days of caricature and polemics appear to be largely behind us. Certainly good will and cooperation between churches have occurred on many critical issues. An obvious commitment to and desire for closer relations, including mutual recognition of ministries and eucharistic sharing, is evident not only in the official documents we have surveyed but also in countless Christian congregations of many denominational labels. Multilateral and bilateral conversations have led to advances in theological understandings that call many of the historic causes of Christian divisiveness into question. If the present moment of ecumenical history reveals little interest in vast organic mergers into structural giants, it also reflects a high degree of impatience with the present state of affairs on the local level. Much of this restlessness is useful in prompting other arenas of the church to take their ecumenical responsibilities more seriously, but sometimes it fails to recognize the complexity of the issues involved. While the churches cannot become complacent about the issue of unity, there needs to be some understanding of what has been achieved. After centuries of divisions and isolation, in a remarkably short time the churches have responded in some significant ways to the movement of the Spirit. Compared to the efforts of the nations of the world to secure disarmament or to guarantee world peace, the ecumenical progress in this century is commendable. Nevertheless the question is valid and urgent. After all the consultations, all the dialogues and documents, can the ecumenical movement expect to make any more progress so that the churches move beyond the present situation into one in which they can be and act more and more as members of the same body of Christ? In brief, does the ecumenical movement have a promise for the future? Granted the churches have journeyed far in this century. Does the road lead farther or are the churches in a cul-de-sac?

Involved in this cogent question is a necessary corollary inquiry: Is there clarity about the goal of the journey? Until we have some goal or vision of its outcome, we cannot know the length of the journey. In the early years of the ecumenical movement it was enough for the churches to know that they were committed to greater expressions of their unity. In fact, if more had been required in those early years, the ecumenical movement might well have floundered. Now, however, greater precision, although not absolute clarity, is required. Much attention has been paid to the need to focus the vision of unity. Part of this effort has necessarily concerned itself with the important distinction between the final goal or vision of unity and the necessary steps on the way.

It has been long recognized in the ecumenical movement that the churches will never move immediately from disunity to unity but will make the change in a series of stages. At least five main steps in this process have been identified and are listed below. These stages are not automatically successive. The various communions will move at different speeds, arriving at different stages of unity with one another in their own time. Even with these cautions, the series of stages listed here does indicate the general direction along the road to ecumenical advance.

- First, competition. Here a church sees itself as entirely self-sufficient and does not acknowledge the role or need of any other church. This could be described as a pre-ecumenical stage.
- Second, coexistence. Here a church begins to acknowledge that Christ can also be known in other churches, but there is no initiative to enter into structural relationships.
- Third, cooperation. Now a church recognizes other churches to the degree that it is able to undertake certain tasks with them.

There is a real, if limited, partnership of churches. Ecumenical concern has come to expression.

- Fourth, commitment. Now there is a recognition that partnership in particular projects does not reflect the degree of mutual recognition that exists between the churches. Thus, the churches enter into general, open-ended agreements to do together many things as members of the same body.
- Finally, communion. Now it no longer makes sense to think of fellowship as consisting of two or more separate entities. Rather, all separation is overcome in the appropriate wholeness and singleness of the body of Christ.

Although this scheme is not ideal, the ability to mark steps on the ecumenical road makes it possible to maintain a dynamism. Churches realize that they are able to mark irreversible steps. There is no way backward without creating new divisions and destroying the newly emerging community. Churches on this road acknowledge that their unity lies before them. It is no longer possible to return to the time before divisions occurred to achieve unity, because in the periods of separation of the churches new questions arose that led to further divisions. The churches in the midst of this ecumenical journey realize that the unity of all Christians is not some optional feature of the nature of the church which, though desirable, can if necessary be dispensed with. Rather, according to the doctrine of the early church, they affirm unity, along with apostolicity and catholicity, as essential to the existence and the nature of the community of the church. This view means that if unity is not realized, the very existence of the church is in question.

As a general statement, open to much qualification, it probably could be maintained that in the mid-1980s many of the churches actively participating in the ecumenical movement are at a stage between cooperation and commitment in their relations with other churches in councils and other ecumenical organizations; and in their relations with other churches with which they are in dialogue, they are at a stage between commitment and communion. This latter comment is certainly true of Anglican–Roman Catholic, Roman Catholic–Lutheran, and Lutheran-Anglican relations in many places.

Recently several models of unity have been offered to the churches for their consideration in this process of steps toward communion, not as final visions of unity in themselves, but as helpful direction posts on the pilgrimage. All of these models share a commitment: real unity in Christ must mean for the churches a unity that is visible and tangible. Unity that is interpreted as an invisible relation, leaving the outward forms of disunited churches unchanged, is not the goal of the ecumenical movement. Such a view does not negate the spiritual dimensions of Christian unity. On the contrary, it affirms them but goes beyond that to say that genuine spirituality acknowledges that a real unity in Christ has to be incarnated in the church's forms and structures. These models also share a common recognition that the structures of unity must be such as to maintain an identifiable continuity with their past so that there will be neither an absorption of one church by another nor a leveling of all churches into a synthetic hybrid. In this regard these newer models stand in contrast to the concept of organic union which for many years was the only vision of the ecumenical movement. Organic union implies that the existence of different church traditions or confessions is a decisive obstacle to unity, and that unity can be realized only by abandoning traditional ecclesial and confessional features. It involves a kind of death of the traditions and confessions that existed previously. If in many ecumenical circles today organic union is out of favor, it is because for many it has come to be seen as a model of unity that does not give attention to the genuine diversity within the Christian tradition.[1]

Three proposed new models are described below. The first, unity as "a communion of communions," was initially proposed by Cardinal Willebrands, president of the Vatican Secretariat for Promoting Christian Unity, and was then taken up within the Anglican communion. Here sister churches, each with its own tradition of theology, liturgy, spirituality, and discipline, live in communion with one another. The second model is unity made "visible in each place and in all places and ages" from the Third Assembly of the World Council of Churches at New Delhi in 1961 which was further elaborated by the Fifth Assembly of the World Council of Churches at Nairobi in 1975 in terms of "conciliar fellowship." The third is the concept of "reconciled diversity" that developed in Lutheran circles and was originally seen as an alternative to the models from the World Council of Churches.

Within the last few years an extremely valuable publication from the Lutheran World Federation has offered a helpful discussion of the "conciliar fellowship" and "reconciled diversity" models, explaining what these conceptions are and how they relate.[2] It is worth examining the major features of this work by Günther Gassmann and Harding Meyer. The authors begin by noting the need for clear concepts of unity. The Creed confesses that the church of Jesus Christ is one. This unity that is part of the church's essence is both a gift and a task. As the ecumenical movement encourages reflection, prayer, and efforts in dialogue and common witness and action, the question arises as to the forms in which unity is to be made visible. Even provisional concepts are of value. The New Testament does not specify a systematic model of unity, and the forms of unity in the ancient church cannot be directly applied to the twentieth century. Still, it is possible in the New Testament to see some basic structures of unity that are of lasting importance: (1) Individual congregations and churches are bound together by one and the same faith and not separated by any divisive differences, (2) they recognize one another as churches in full fellowship, and (3) this unity finds expression in common life, mutual aid, and joint consultation and decision making.

Gassmann and Meyer observe that these structures of unity had their center in agreement concerning the preaching of the gospel and the administration of the sacrament, items expressed in Article 7 of the Augsburg Confession. Thus Lutherans have come to insist that, although there is no distinctively Lutheran model of unity, any form of visible manifestation of church unity must include agreement on the basic elements of the apostolic and catholic faith. For Lutherans this means that agreement can take the form of common consensus statements, joint recognition of confessions of doctrine and of the way of faith expressed in practice.

Then Gassmann and Meyer examine the concepts of unity that have been conceived in the studies of the World Council of Churches and articulated in the reports of three assemblies. These texts are so important that they deserve quotation.

> We believe that the unity which is both God's will and his gift to his church is being made visible as all in each place who are baptized into Jesus Christ and confess him as Lord and Saviour are brought by the Holy Spirit into one fully committed fellowship holding the one apostolic faith, preaching the one gospel, breaking the one bread, joining in common prayer, and having a corporate life reaching out in witness and service to all, and who at the same time are united with the whole Christian fellowship in all places and in all ages in such wise that ministry and members are accepted by all, and that all can act and speak together as occasion requires for the tasks to which God calls his people.[3]

> Yet it is within this very world that God makes catholicity available to men through the ministry of Christ in his Church. The purpose of Christ is to bring people of all times, of all races, of all places, of all conditions, into an organic and living unity in Christ by the Holy Spirit under the universal fatherhood of God. This unity is not solely external; it has a deeper internal dimension, which is also expressed by the term "catholicity." Catholicity reaches its completion when what God has already begun in history is finally disclosed and fulfilled.[4]

> Catholicity is a gift of the Spirit, but it is also a task, a call and engagement.[5]

> The Church is bold in speaking of itself as the sign of the coming unity of humankind.[6]

> The one Church is to be envisioned as a conciliar fellowship of local churches which are themselves united. In this conciliar fellowship each local church possesses in communion with the others, the fulness of catholicity, witnesses to the same apostolic faith and therefore recognizes the others as belonging to the same church of Christ and guided by the same Spirit. They are bound together because they have received the same doctrine, and share in the same eucharist; they recognize each other's members and ministries. They are one in their common commitment to confess the gospel of Christ by proclamation and service to the world. To this end, each church aims at maintaining sustained and sustaining relationships with her sister churches in conciliar gatherings whenever required for the fulfillment of their common calling.[7]

"Conciliar fellowship," as the Lutheran World Federation publication states, is not the official unity concept of the World Council of

Churches, but it does express elements generally recognized as indispensable for church unity. These include common confession of the apostolic faith; mutual recognition of apostolicity and catholicity of other churches and of members, sacraments, and ministries; fellowship in the Lord's Supper and in mission and service in the world; and the achievement of mutual fellowship.[8]

The major problem identified with this picture of unity is that it rests too exclusively on the older model of organic union with its idea that divided local congregations and local churches should surrender their confessional traditions and identities to constitute a single church. This model leaves little room for confessionally defined traditions or the enrichment they could bring. This approach is in contrast to the goal of the dialogues that have sought to achieve theological agreement while not necessarily eliminating all differences between churches and confessions or ending in church union. The theological agreement of the dialogues attempts to overcome the divisive character of existing differences in order to allow full fellowship. The dialogues, therefore, seemed to call into question the concept of unity emerging from the World Council of Churches.

The concept arising from the dialogues came to be known as "reconciled diversity." The key idea here is that confessional traditions and identities are not surrendered but that existing differences between churches lose their divisive character by being transformed, changed, and renewed in the process of bilateral conversation. Thus a reconciliation, not a leveling out of differences, occurs. From this a vision of unity develops that has the character of a "reconciled diversity."

Between 1973 and 1978 a number of meetings were held dealing with these two concepts of "conciliar fellowship" and "reconciled diversity." From the outset supporters of the latter idea insisted that it was to be seen as complementary and corrective to "conciliar fellowship" and not a rival. At its 1977 Assembly the Lutheran World Federation encouraged the understanding of unity that allows room for the diversity of confessional traditions and the existence of fellowships to cherish these traditions. Although sometimes misunderstood, the intention of "reconciled diversity" was never simply to preserve and maintain confessional differences. The Assembly be-

121

lieved "reconciled diversity" comes close to the concept of "conciliar fellowship" except that the latter term does not take seriously enough confessional differences and the need to preserve them. The Assembly stated that the concept of "reconciled diversity" in itself does not provide a detailed and final description of the goal of unity.[9]

As Gassmann and Meyer describe, by 1978 a fundamental clarification of the relation of concepts of unity had been achieved.[10] This clarification contained the following points. There are four basic requirements for the unity of the church: (1) the ending of prejudices, hostilities, and lifting of condemnations; (2) the sharing of one faith; (3) the mutual recognition of baptism, Eucharist, and ministry; and (4) the agreement on ways of deciding and acting together.

The vision of the one church as a "conciliar fellowship of local churches which are themselves truly united" is regarded as a further elaboration of the concept of the organic unity of the church as the body of Christ, the manifold *koinonia* of the New Testament and church fathers. "Unity in reconciled diversity" and "organic unity" are two different but legitimate forms of local churches truly united.

This review gives us a good insight into recent ecumenical thinking about the vision of unity. That the ecumenical movement does not yet have a full vision of the unity it is seeking is not entirely bad. The ecumenical movement is *in via;* it has a pilgrim character. Thus it must have a certain tentativeness so that it has the freedom to respond to the Spirit. On the other hand, enough clarity has been reached, so that certain characteristics of the form of visible unity are becoming sharper and distinct. The emerging view of visible unity is one of the promises of the ecumenical movement for the future.

Another issue on which the promise of the ecumenical movement will depend is the topic becoming known as "reception." I have defined "reception" to include all the phases and aspects of a process by which a church makes the result of bilateral or multilateral conversation a part of its faith and life.[11] Reception in this sense is a new situation for the churches. It has arisen because after years of appointing official representatives to bilateral and multilateral conversations a considerable amount of theological agreement has been produced. As we saw in chapter 5, these statements of agreement have implications for the relationships between churches. The churches are asked, in effect, by these agreements to have their faith and life touched at the deepest levels. The churches are requested to accept and make their own something that they did not produce alone. In a sense, these ecumenical agreements come from outside the churches and they make claims on the churches. The question before all the churches is the degree to which they are prepared to make authoritative within their own life the conclusions of the dialogues. This question in turn raises the questions of how the churches teach authoritatively today. If they wish to come to such decisions and receive the work of the dialogue, how do they do it? Reception is a complex phenomenon that has several aspects. Reception is not merely an administrative or intellectual step. The competent and official authorities of the church are involved, but so are local congregations in their worship and life. All concerned in the churches will need to see that the apostolicity and catholicity of the church are intimately associated. Reception for any church raises two related questions: (1) Is what is being received in full harmony with the apostolic faith as the church has received it and (2) what should be done in and between the churches involved if they have been able to answer the first question affirmatively? Of course, the process of reception begins initially with the decision to enter into a dialogue. Obviously a certain sense of recognition of both parties as church is required for dialogue to begin. The scandal of division and the need to do something about it are acknowledged. But if the dialogue has done its work well, the agreement will be saying something new. There may be new language, new emphases, and new insights. It is precisely all of this that must be examined by the churches as they seek to answer those two questions. After centuries of divisions it is not realistic to expect that this process will be swift or simple. At this juncture of history it is probably critical that steps be taken which will both signal and encourage progress along the path to unity. The responsible step that certain Lutheran churches and the Episcopal Church were able to take offers such encouragement and places further dialogues in a new context. It may be hoped that other such steps will be possible, perhaps as a result of the study of the reports of the Anglican–Roman Catholic International Commission.

It is clear that if the churches involved in the major dialogue activity to date (especially, but not exclusively, Anglicans, Lutherans, Orthodox, and Roman Catholics) would receive the results of the dialogues in which they have taken part, these churches could move a significant way toward unity. The conviction of some scholars is that the dialogues have already solved the major issues that have kept the churches apart for centuries. The challenge, then, is not to find solutions but to have those solutions be decisive in the life and faith of the churches. Put another way, the question is, What degree of pluralism is acceptable for the churches? Only the churches can answer that question. While it is not possible in an uncritical way simply to return to some earlier century of church history, many ecumenists today believe that the early church has potential as an ecumenical model, for the early church allowed considerable diversity in tension with unity. Edmund Schlink has argued this point in regard to problems of church order and dogma. He has said:

> In both these areas, the Primitive Church shows a much greater diversity of thought and definition than is shown in the later history of dogma and canon law, and greater than most would feel to be reconcilable with the future unity of the Church in the midst of the divisions of the churches. It is only with the regaining of this type of fellowship that we can understand the unity of the Early Church, and what has been scattered during the course of Church History can be brought back once more into a new and close unity.[12]

In Europe in 1983 two veteran Roman Catholic ecumenists, Heinrich Fries and Karl Rahner, published a book that caused interest and excitement. The English edition published in 1985 is entitled *Unity of the Churches—An Actual Possibility.*[13] The book has one basic thesis: enough theological agreement has been reached between the churches that, if they are prepared to live with a level of pluralism no greater than that now found within the churches, unity, including pulpit and altar fellowship, is presently possible. Fries and Rahner have put before the churches a sharp summons to take seriously the work of contemporary biblical and historical study and of the dialogues, and in fact to receive it. Their book is a concrete reminder that in part the promise of the ecumenical movement for the future is related to how quickly the churches will engage in the process of reception. The process will not be uniform. Different communions will progress at different rates of speed. For all churches it will at times be painful. Reception risks producing new tensions and even divisions. Though churches have already indicated that it will be a difficult task, they have also offered ample proof that they are prepared responsibly to face it. There is one more reason why the ecumenical movement has promise for the future.

Before leaving the topic of reception, we should make special mention of the challenge of reception as it relates to one ecumenical document, *Baptism, Eucharist and Ministry.*[14] This text, produced by the Commission on Faith and Order after some fifty-five years of work, claims an ecumenical convergence on three crucial ecumenical subjects. Over one hundred theologians—Roman Catholic, Orthodox, Lutheran, Anglican, and others—considered this text to have reached a sufficient stage of maturity that they transmitted it to the churches, asking them to do two things. The churches are requested to take up the question of reception involving the whole people of God and all levels of church life. This is a long-term process—in fact, a commitment to a long-term goal. The churches are also asked to prepare an official response to *Baptism, Eucharist and Ministry* at their highest level of authority. "Response" is carefully distinguished from the process of "reception." Originally the churches were asked to give a response by 31 December, 1984, but this date was later changed to 31 December, 1985. Several churches, including the Lutheran Church in America, have already made their official response. The Commission on Faith and Order did not ask the churches to comment on the text, but put four specific questions to them: (1) To what extent can a church recognize in this text the faith of the church through the ages? (2) What consequences can it draw from this text for its relations and dialogues with other churches? (3) What guidance can a church take from this text for its worship and for its educational, ethical, and spiritual life and witness? (4) What suggestions can a church make for the ongoing work of Faith and Order? *Baptism, Eucharist and Ministry* asks all the churches to affirm the sacraments as effective signs of God's grace of salvation: (1) baptism (believer's or infant) as unrepeatable incorporation into the church; (2) the Eucharist as invoked by the Spirit, actualized memorial, sacrifice of praise, and communion celebrated weekly; and (3) the apostolic tradition with its presbyterial and episcopal succession, the threefold ministry as a full sign of continuity and unity, and a universal priesthood of the baptized. If churches are able to respond positively to this Faith and Order text and sustain within themselves the momentum of the process of reception, what may occur is a constellation of churches finding greater expressions of visible unity around the convergence claimed in *Baptism, Eucharist and Ministry*. This would be a significant ecumenical advance having implications even for those churches which initially had difficulty in accepting the *Baptism, Eucharist and Ministry* convergence as their own. Thus by stimulating the churches to reflect on the faith of the church through the ages, this document gives new promise to the future of the ecumenical movement. If, finally, the churches can receive *Baptism, Eucharist and Ministry*, an essential ecclesiality will be reached. But it is too early to predict what will occur. Perhaps the first opportunity to judge the extent to which *Baptism, Eucharist and Ministry* has advanced the churches toward the mutual recognition of baptism, Eucharist, and ministries will be at the projected fifth world conference on Faith and Order tentatively scheduled to meet in 1988 or early 1989 and have before it the official responses of the churches.

A number of other items all bear on the promise of the ecumenical movement for the future. While all cannot be discussed here at a length appropriate to their importance, they do deserve special mention. One such item is the role of the Roman Catholic Church in the ecumenical movement. As we described earlier, the Roman Catholic Church has entered into the ecumenical movement in ways quite unpredictable prior to 1962. The reversal of earlier policy was seen most dramatically in the Second Vatican Council. Since that time, ecumenical progress within the Roman Catholic Church has been great, although uneven. In the 1980s a dilemma of a special nature has occurred. It may be put as simply as this: Has the Roman Catholic Church proceeded about as far as it can go ecumenically on the basis of the documents of the Second Vatican Council? We have already observed that the Decree on Ecumenism in many ways reflects where the ecumenical movement was in the 1960s. Certainly the spirit of Vatican II gives some clear hints for future ecumenical progress. But how is this dilemma resolved if the Roman Catholic Church, or its leadership, concludes that on the basis of the actual conciliar texts, there is not the possibility to go forward? Reception of ecumenical dialogues, steps on the way to unity, and the implications of the 450th anniversary of the Augsburg Confession and of the 500th anniversary of the birth of Martin Luther are new ecumenical items to which the Second Vatican Council could not speak. There is more and more discussion in Roman Catholic circles about the need for another council by the end of the twentieth century to receive these newer ecumenical items into the life and faith of the Roman Catholic Church as the Second Vatican Council received the ecumenical movement for the Roman Catholic Church. Admittedly some of this is speculative, but the promise of the ecumenical movement for the future will hang, in some ways, on how the Roman Catholic Church is able to give some signal in the near future, by concrete steps, that the ecumenical progress since the 1960s will in some measure be acknowledged and appreciated.

Another item that will have a bearing on the ecumenical future is the role of councils of churches. We can think here especially of the World Council of Churches and the National Council of the Churches of Christ in the U.S.A. In the course of their histories such organizations have undergone some changes. Most conciliar organizations began as vehicles for cooperation between churches. Assigned little authority by the churches, they were viewed as agencies for cooperative work. But as commitment has grown in the churches and theological issues become less divisive, councils have begun to change. Though they do not become churches, they have exhibited the desire to transform themselves so that they can be arenas in which the churches express their unity. Often they wish to take on some characteristics of churches or at least underscore the ecclesiastical implications of membership in them. In the 1980s councils are in the process of change. At their best they do not wish to be rivals to the churches but facilitators of the churches' cooperative work and expressions of unity. Within recent years the National Council of Churches has changed from understanding itself to be a "cooperative agency" to seeing itself as "a community of communions." It is not exactly certain what this latter term means. Not everyone would offer the same exegesis of the phrase, but the intention behind the expression is clear. It wants to assert that when churches join the National Council of Churches they are not joining an organization for cooperation but a community of other churches. This has some implications for their relations with one another. This characteristic became especially clear at the Assembly of the Lutheran World Federation in Budapest in 1984. For the first time the member churches of the Lutheran World Federation declared that because of their membership in this organization they are in pulpit and altar fellowship with one another. It is not clear where this evolution of ecumenical, conciliar organizations will finally go, but it is obvious that this time of ferment for councils is part of the promise of the future in the ecumenical movement.

Finally one area of the ecumenical scene that relates directly to the future of ecumenism must be mentioned. It is so critical to the movement that it deserves special treatment in its own right. Here we will be able to comment on only some of its more important features. The topic is local ecumenism, a subject too often ignored—usually because of two false impressions: (1) that the important arenas of ecumenism are elsewhere, and (2) that it is difficult to observe what is happening ecumenically on the local scene. Neither assumption is necessarily correct. Local ecumenism is best defined as ecumenism that occurs in congregations or parishes in areas where Christians live with one another in communities or other groups.[15]

The factors that motivate local ecumenism are similar to those that promote ecumenism regionally, nationally, or institutionally, although the stress or accent is often different. For example, social factors clearly motivate local ecumenism. The challenge of a pluralistic society and the concrete social and ethical problems of daily life can often be the cause for joint action by Christians of different traditions. Emergency situations, such as natural catastrophes, can encourage Christians in an area to cooperate. This cooperation often leads to commitments and the reduction of prejudices which have implications for unity. The new knowledge and new understandings that personal and community experiences engender appear to influence local ecumenism more directly than international ecumenical efforts. Yet such motivations, while effective in many places, are often unarticulated. Perhaps the strongest local motivation is the desire of

Christians to see a renewal of the church where they live. They wish for a renewal of the church that includes the longing for a strengthened and lived communion within the individual church and beyond its denominational boundaries. Connected with this, in the opinion of many persons, is the hope for a stronger influence of local churches and an increase in the church's credibility. For many it is linked with the question of survival. Local churches must learn to express their oneness. Still it appears that such hopes are not realized in many local situations. The explanation for this is probably that ecumenical concern, even when it has approval, is generally not regarded as a necessary and constitutive element of parish life, but as an extra burden or one activity among many. Whether much happens in a particular situation seems often, in the final analysis, to depend on the ecumenical consciousness of those responsible for parishes.

In spite of the fact that we live in times that stress the role of the whole people of God in the life of the church, local ecumenism depends to a large degree on local clergy. Without the participation of local clergy, local ecumenism languishes. Critical here are the self-understanding of the local clergy and their priorities. Too often the clergy view ecumenism as a means of promoting revival and a deepening of parish life. It is seen only as a means of achieving success. But although ecumenical sensationalism can bring headlines, it leaves few lasting results. For some clergy it becomes a question of priorities. Ecumenism is seen as an additional workload and therefore is given little attention. Still there are other local clergy who will invest much time and energy in the ecumenical task, even when the fruits do not immediately correspond to the efforts. But the great influence of the clergy on local ecumenism remains critical. In numerous situations it can be shown that the change of a pastor for a parish can mean a sudden change in the ecumenical attitude of the parish. If a pastor who is strongly motivated ecumenically is followed by someone more cautious, or vice versa, the parish will often change its ecumenical orientation quickly. If the local pastor sees himself or herself as a mediator and translator of ecumenism in other arenas of the church's life to the local scene and has good personal relations with other local clergy, local ecumenism will prosper. Otherwise it will not.

At first glance we might be tempted to think that the vision of unity described early in this chapter would not play a major role in local ecumenism. This is not, in fact, the case. Lack of ecumenical motivation and the decision not to enter into ecumenical activities is often based on a misunderstanding of the goal of the movement. Unity is frequently assumed to be uniformity and the surrender of present identity. As a more positive understanding of diversity is developed, and often this is not easy to accomplish, then appreciation for the ecumenical movement grows. On the local scene there seems to be a general aversion to the merger of the institutional churches. Supporters and representatives of local ecumenism encourage rather the idea of community or family, stressing that the churches in the ecumenical movement do not wish to attain unity through the elimination of all differences or understand church unity in terms of the mergers of institutions. The family can be understood as a trustworthy community in which the differences of individual members can be accepted as long as they do not break up the family or threaten its basic unity. When such a view is presented as compatible with the ecumenical movement, local interest increases. In all of this there is always the need to keep alive in the local consciousness the concept of unity of the church as binding beyond the local place and time.

Often it is repeated that doctrinal questions have little significance for local ecumenism. The issue is not that simple. The problem is not the importance or unimportance of doctrinal factors locally; it is, rather, the understanding of doctrine. By "doctrine" theologians mean loyalty to the apostolic heritage, historical continuity, and consensus in the church. Locally it is not understood this way. Locally "doctrine" is thought of as theologically formulated teachings of a normative character, comparable to a kind of law. Persons on the local scene think these doctrines are stifling or detrimental to local ecumenical endeavors. But even when ecumenically local relationships are directed to cooperative activities, questions of joint worship and eucharistic sharing become central points. Local groups do want a common confession of faith, and they hope it will be accepted by the leadership of the churches. As they study questions of Christian responsibility in the world, they address the topic of the witness of the gospel to the world. The relationship of Christian teaching and joint Christian work cannot be avoided. Traditional doctrinal questions may appear in a different form and with different nuances in the local setting, but they are there. For example, the transitional question of Christ's real presence in the Eucharist may be rarely asked, but the problem of what to do with leftover elements often arises. The traditional doctrinal and controversial questions are formulated differently here, but they are present. Other examples regarding the office of the ministry or mixed marriages could be mentioned. All of this increases the importance of bringing about the necessary connection between the ecumenical dialogues and local ecumenism. There must be a recognition of the particularity of the interest and perspectives both of the dialogues and of local ecumenism. The local setting should appreciate that the concern for achieving a responsible theological agreement is required for a genuine and lasting fellowship. Those with responsibility for the theological conversations should be conscious that the needs of local ecumenism are properly directed to the concrete, lived fellowship and that the traditional questions of theology are expressed as relevant only within these perspectives. Much more sharing between the two arenas of ecumenism is needed, and happily there are indications that it is beginning to occur.

Local ecumenism, as other ecumenical arenas, is influenced by nondoctrinal factors. Ethnic or cultural identities, languages, social groups, ideologies, economic conditions, education, political positions, and personal relations influence local ecumenical work. These factors usually are ambivalent in their ecumenical significance. Depending upon the area or situation, the same fact can be either a help or a hindrance toward unity. These factors tend not to remain static but are in a dynamic process of development. Their importance can change quickly. Thus they need closer attention not only on the local level but in the bilateral conversations.

The ecumenical movement on the local scene, as elsewhere in the life of the churches, will always exhibit signs of discouragement and encouragement. It will never be for the impatient. What will help determine the promise of the ecumenical movement for the future will be the attitudes and changes of hearts within the churches. The "data" of some sixty years of study and prayer are there if the churches are willing to make them their own. If they do, the promise of ecumenical movement will be bright. Yet it must always be remembered that the ecumenical movement in the final analysis is not a human enterprise. It is a gift of the Spirit, of a God who continually surprises his people.

As Willem Visser 't Hooft, that great ecumenical veteran to whom the movement toward Christian unity owes so much, once said:

> There is a future for the ecumenical movement provided it does not cease to reflect on its true raison d'être, and draws its life from the heart of the Gospel. Thus the movement will be moving forward. Then the Holy Spirit will work among the churches, taking us and our churches by the neck, driving and binding us together, and thus enabling us to carry out the renewing and saving task in the world.[16]

## NOTES

1. For a supportive view of the concept of organic union, see Paul A. Crow, Jr., *Christian Unity: Matrix for Mission* (New York: Friendship Press, 1982), 102–4.

2. Günther Gassmann and Harding Meyer, *The Unity of the Church: Requirements and Structure* (Geneva: Lutheran World Federation, 1983).

3. W. A. Visser 't Hooft, ed., *The New Delhi Report: The Third Assembly of the World Council of Churches, 1961* (London: SCM Press, 1962), 116.

4. Norman Goodall, ed., *The Uppsala Report, 1968* (Geneva: World Council of Churches, 1968), 13.

5. Ibid.

6. Ibid., 17.

7. David M. Paton, ed., *Breaking Barriers, Nairobi, 1975* (London: S.P.C.K.; Grand Rapids: Wm. B. Eerdmans Publishing Co., 1976), 60.

8. Gassmann and Meyer, *The Unity of the Church*, 5.

9. Arne Sovik, ed., *Proceedings of the Sixth Assembly of the Lutheran World Federation, June 13–26, 1977, Tanzania* (Geneva: Lutheran World Federation, 1977), 173–75, and 200.

10. Gassmann and Meyer, *The Unity of the Church*, 15–18.

11. William G. Rusch, "Baptism, Eucharist and Ministry—and Reception," *Journal of Ecumenical Studies* 21, 1 (1984): 140–44.

12. Edmund Schlink, *The Coming Christ and the Coming Church* (Philadelphia: Fortress Press, 1967), 233.

13. Heinrich Fries and Karl Rahner, *Unity of the Churches—An Actual Possibility* (Philadelphia: Fortress Press, 1985).

14. *Baptism, Eucharist and Ministry,* Faith and Order Paper 111 (Geneva: World Council of Churches, 1982).

15. See the excellent study of this topic by the Institute for Ecumenical Research, Strasbourg, on which the description here is based. André Birmelé, ed., *Local Ecumenism: How Church Unity Is Seen and Practiced by Congregations* (Geneva: World Council of Churches, 1984).

16. W. A. Visser 't Hooft, *Has the Ecumenical Movement a Future?* (Belfast: Christian Journals Limited, 1974), 97.